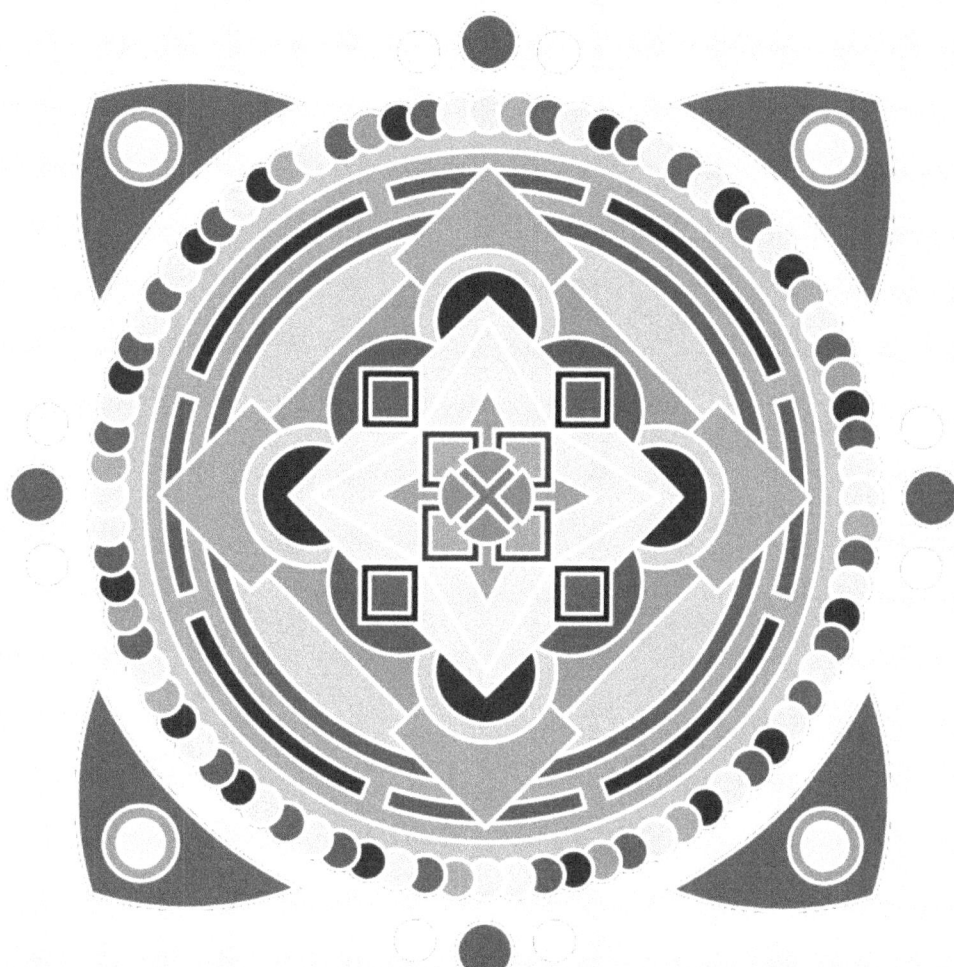

BRING ME TO LIFE COLORING BOOK :

MANDALA

Jessie Shergold

Bring Me To Life
Coloring Book: Mandala

Author: Jessie Shergold

Printed in the United States of America
1st printing June 2016

Bring Me To Life
Coloring Book: Mandala

Introduction:

"Bring Me To Life Coloring Book: Mandala" is a fun and relaxing THEMED coloring book for adults that contains over 30 colorable images for your delight.

Whether you consider yourself artistic or not, coloring for adults can be a very soothing activity. It can help you unwind from a stressful day while bringing out your fun creative side.

There are no 'wrong' color choices. Let your imagination flow and create your own unique interpretation of the mandala images that follow. Tap into your inner child and color away to your heart's content.

Grab a cup of your favorite drink, curl up in your favorite quiet corner, and turn the page to your next exciting coloring subject.

Enjoy!

"Looking at beauty in the world, is the first step of purifying the mind."

~Amit Ray, Meditation: Insights and Inspirations

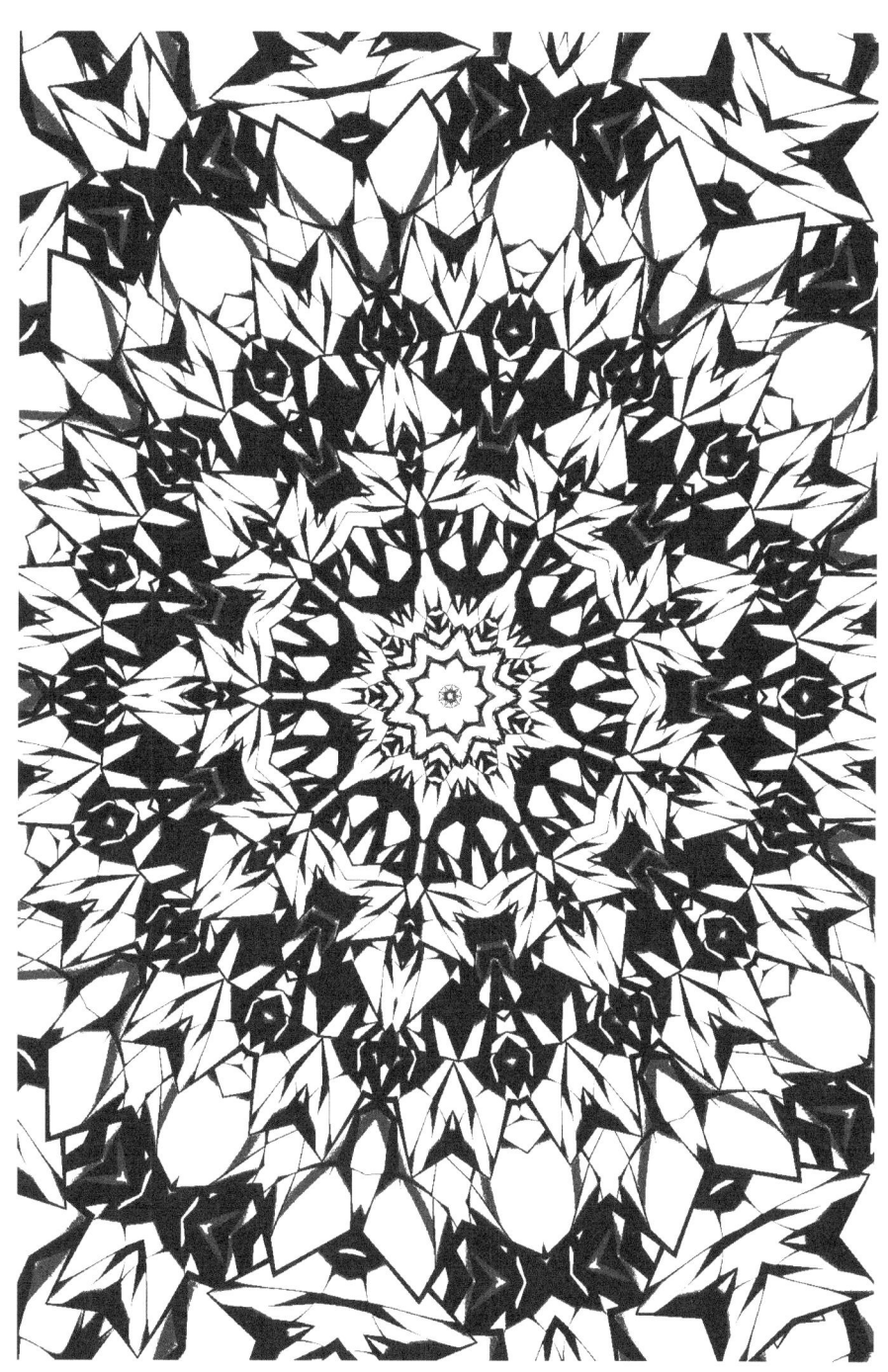

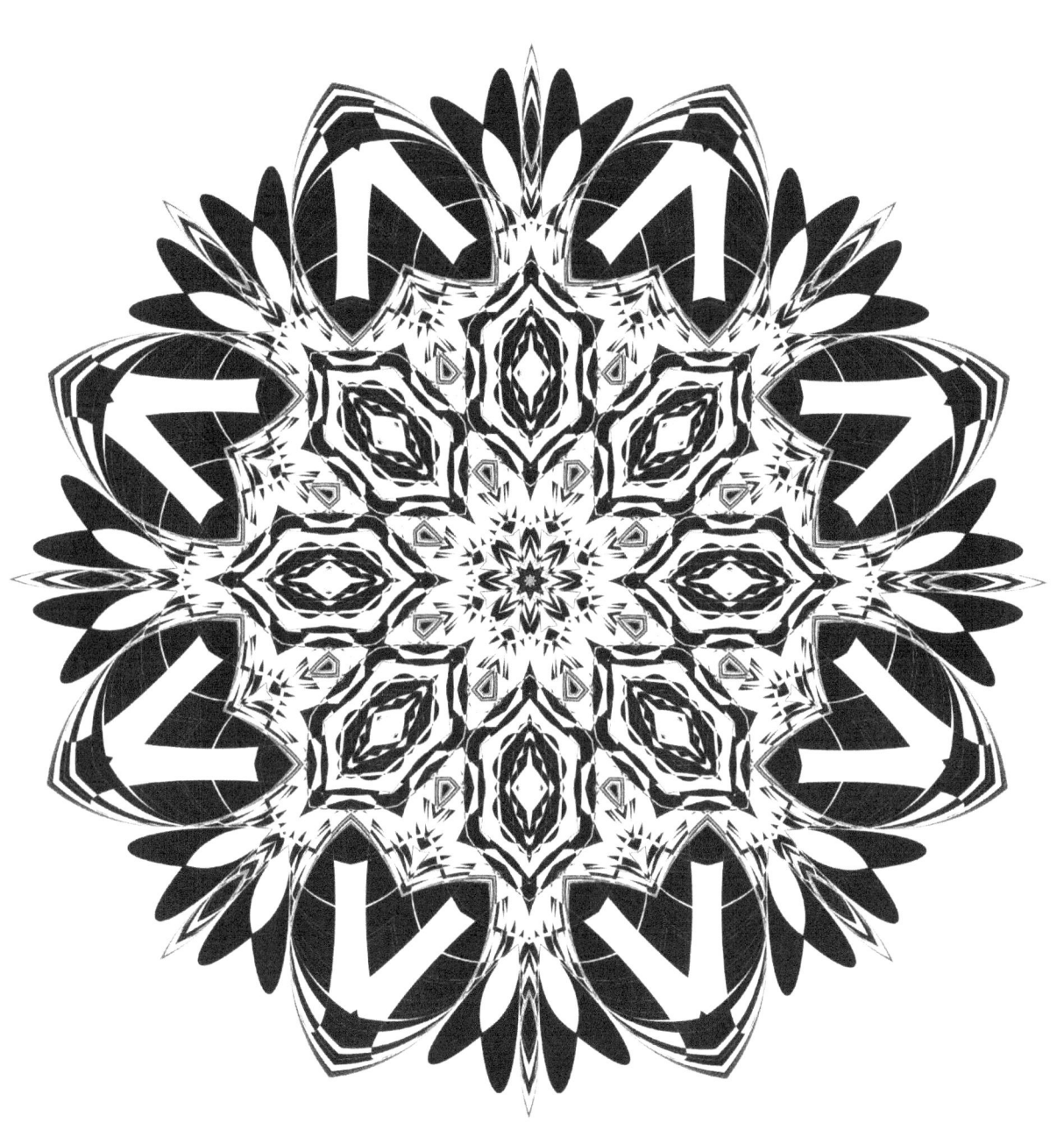

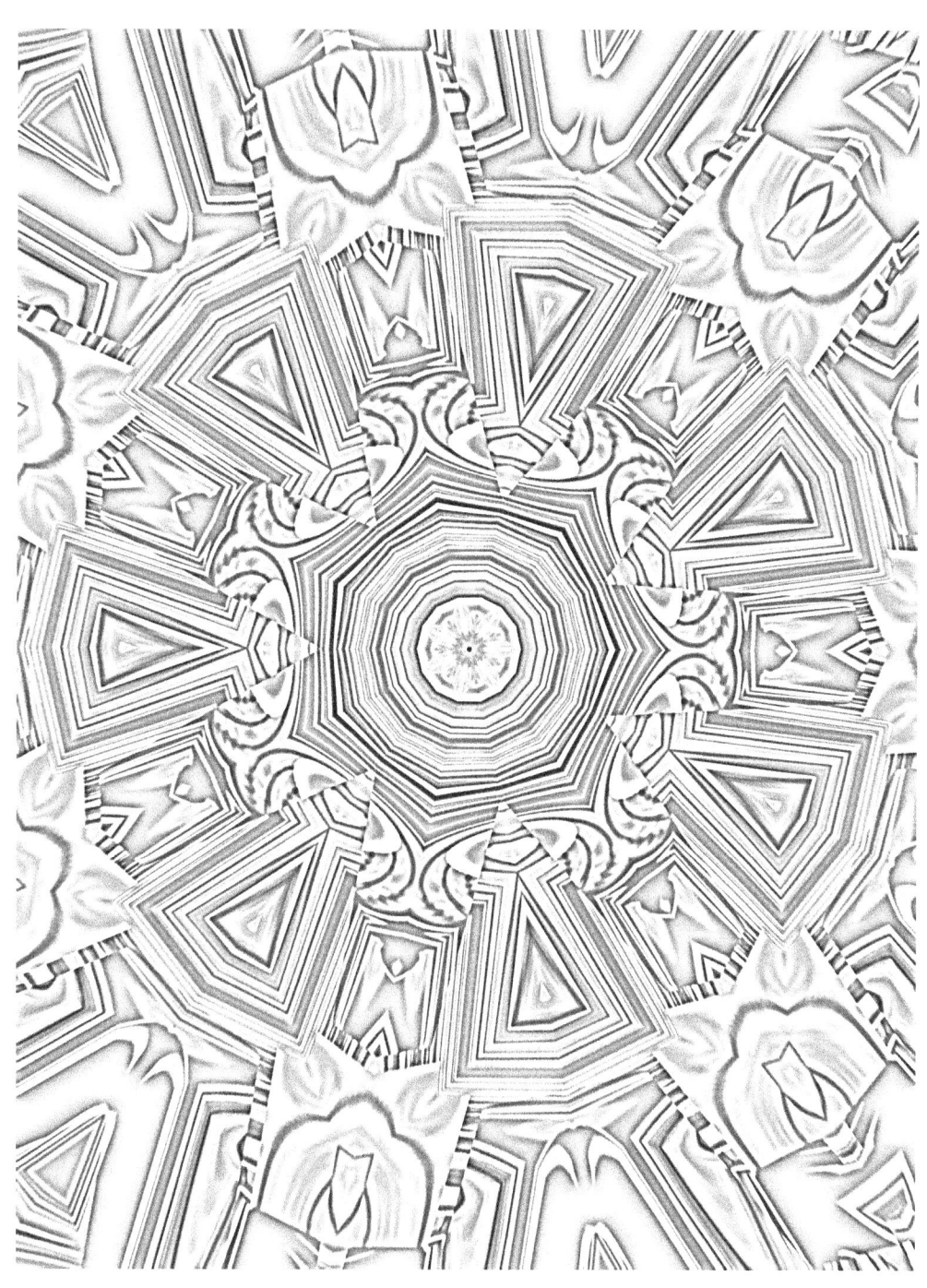

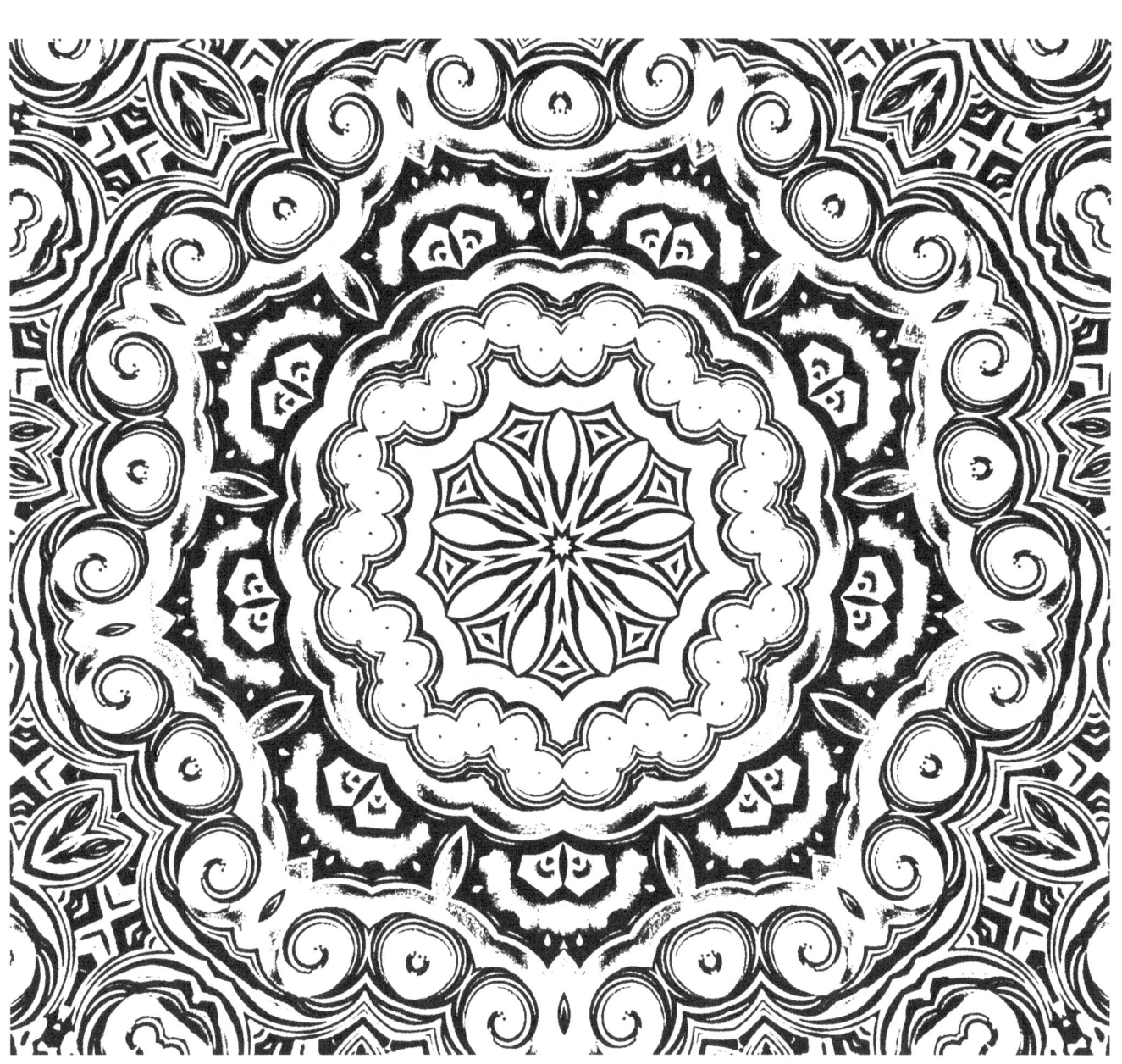

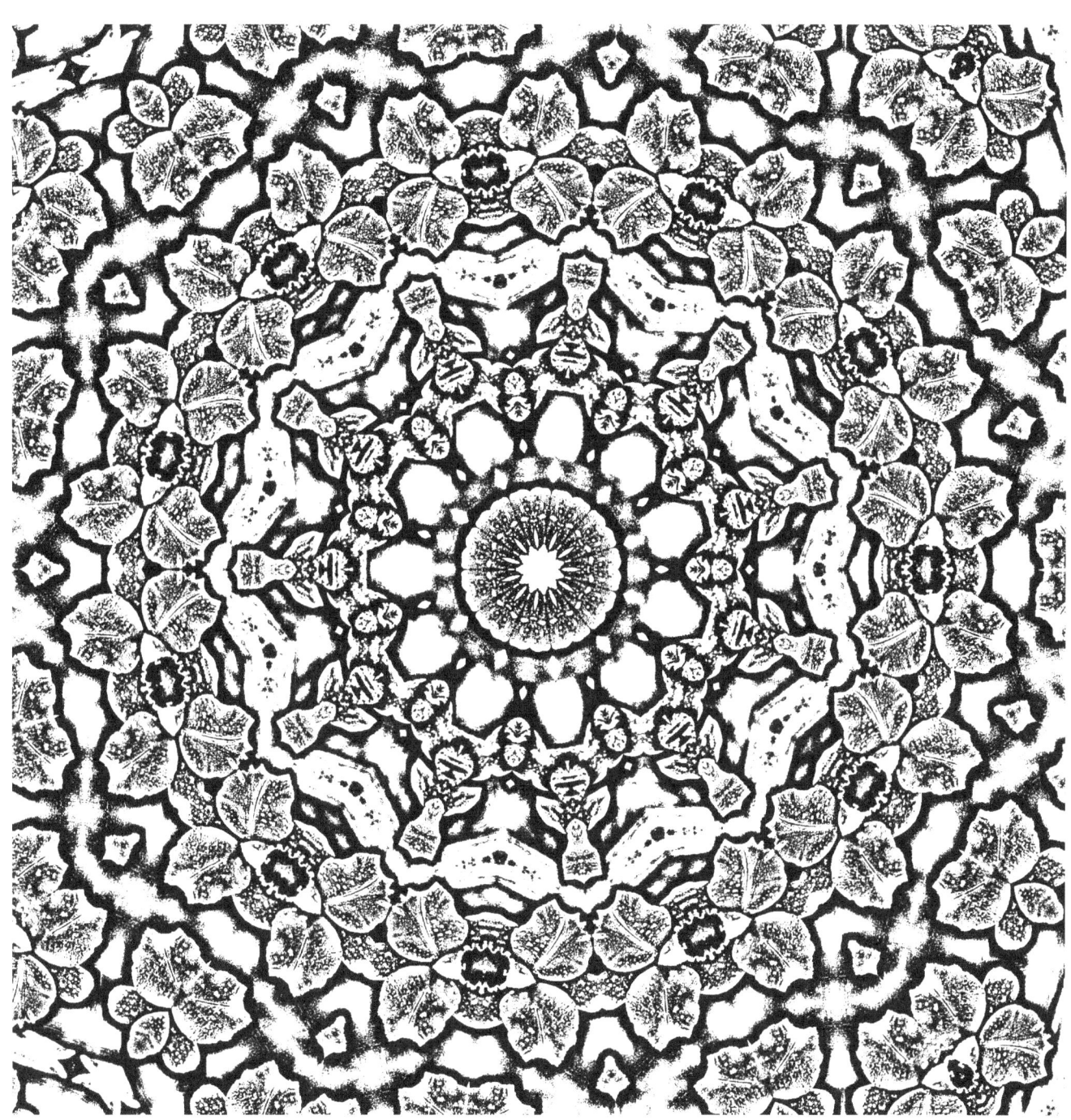

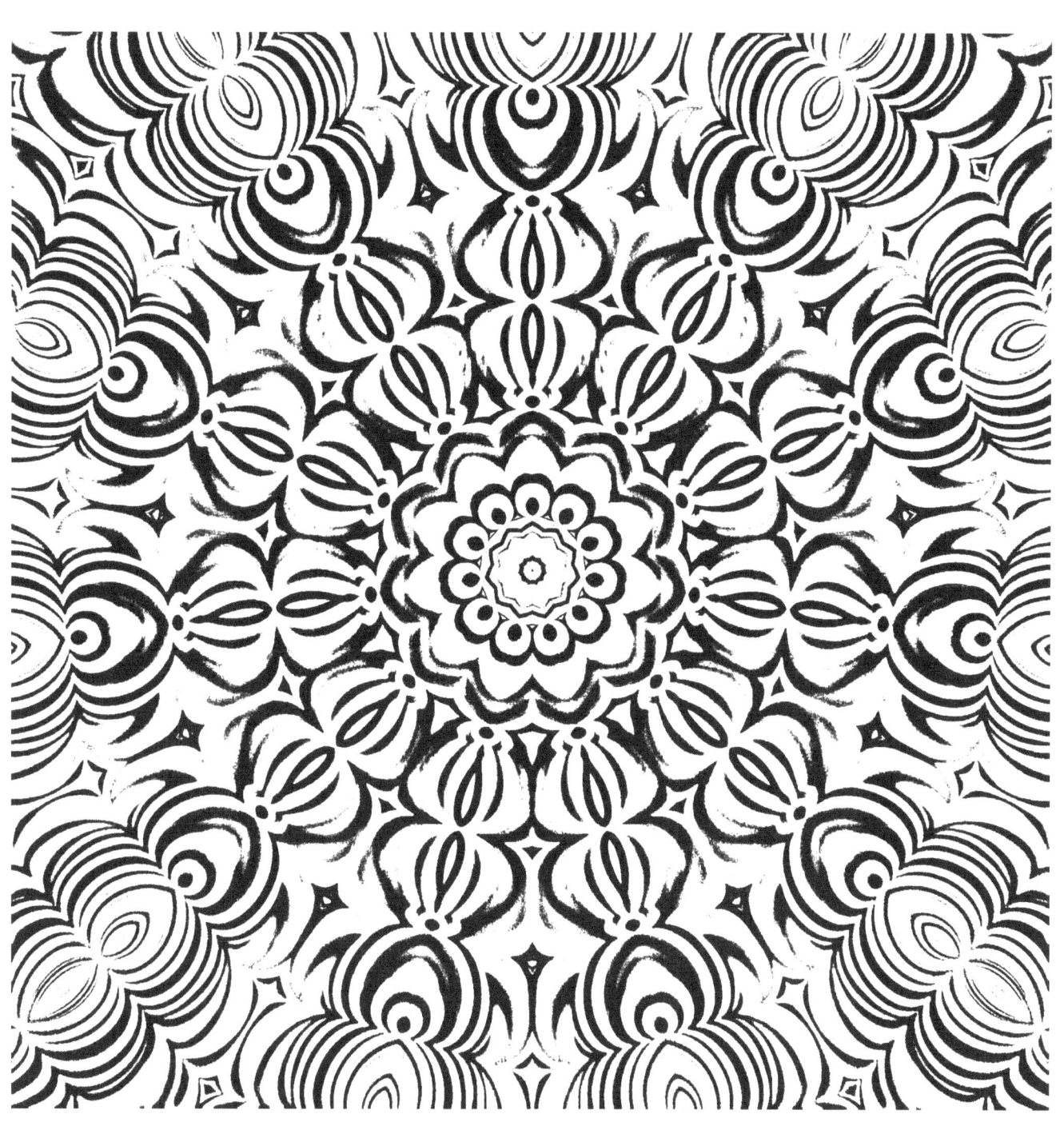

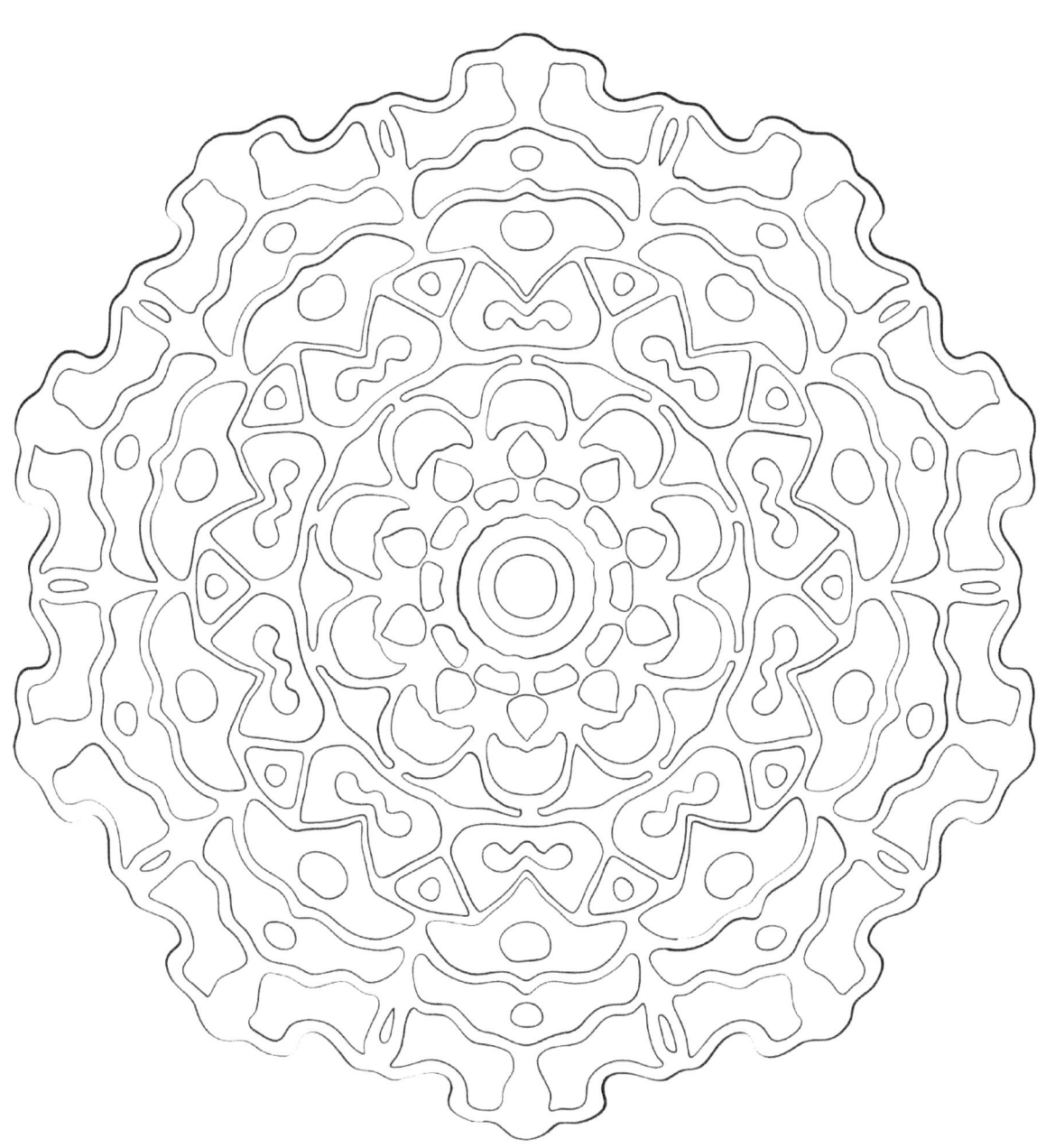

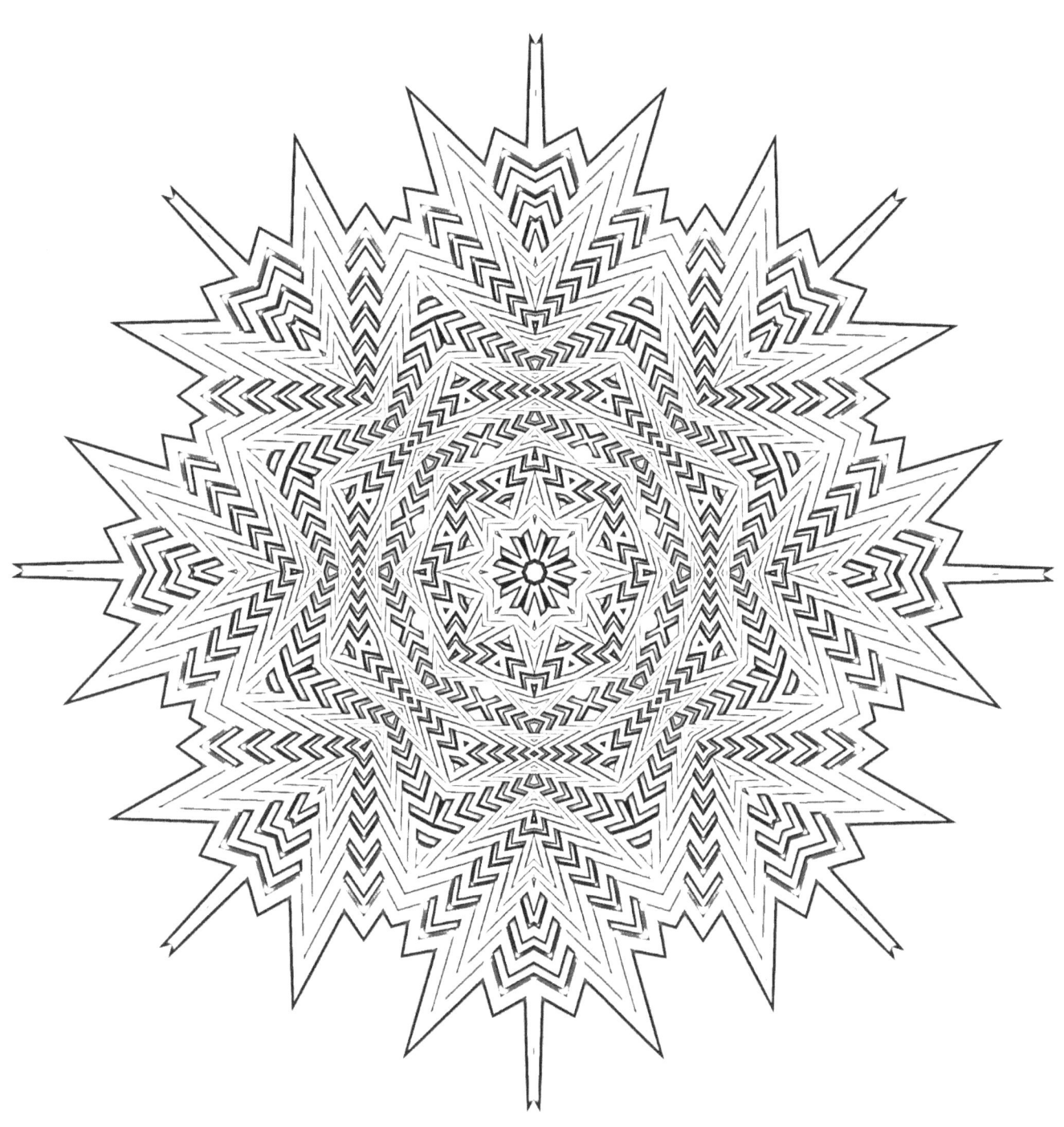

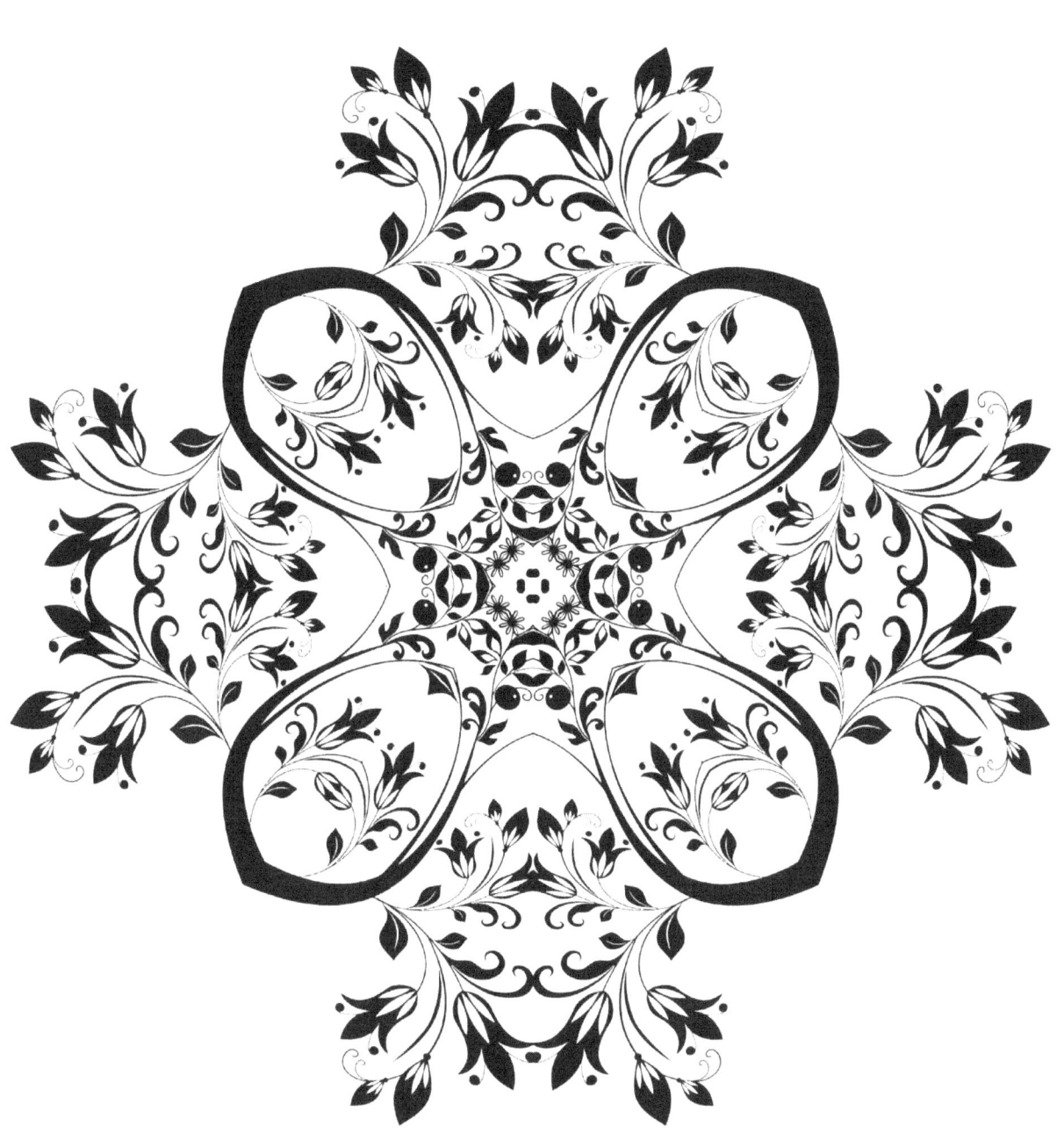

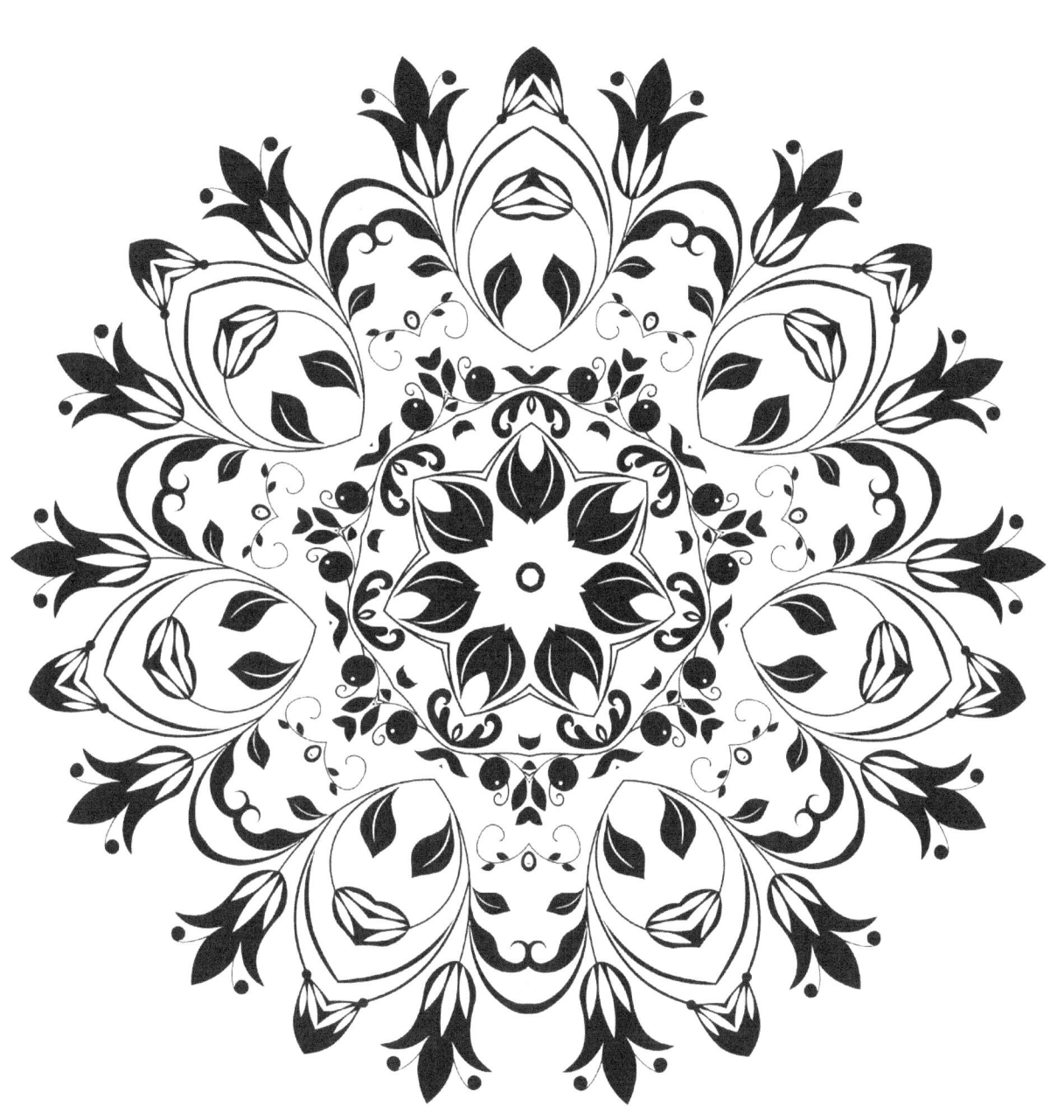

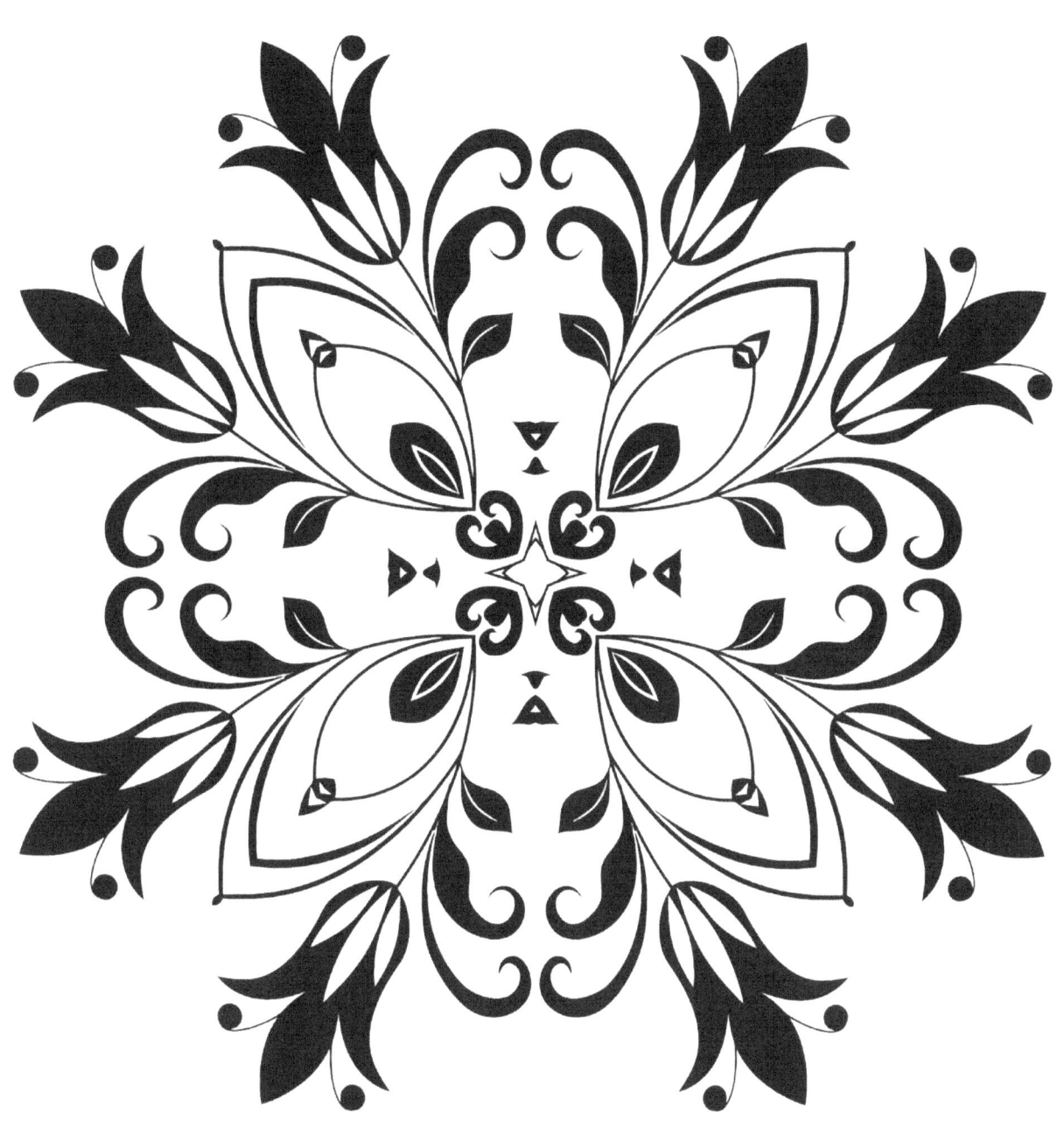

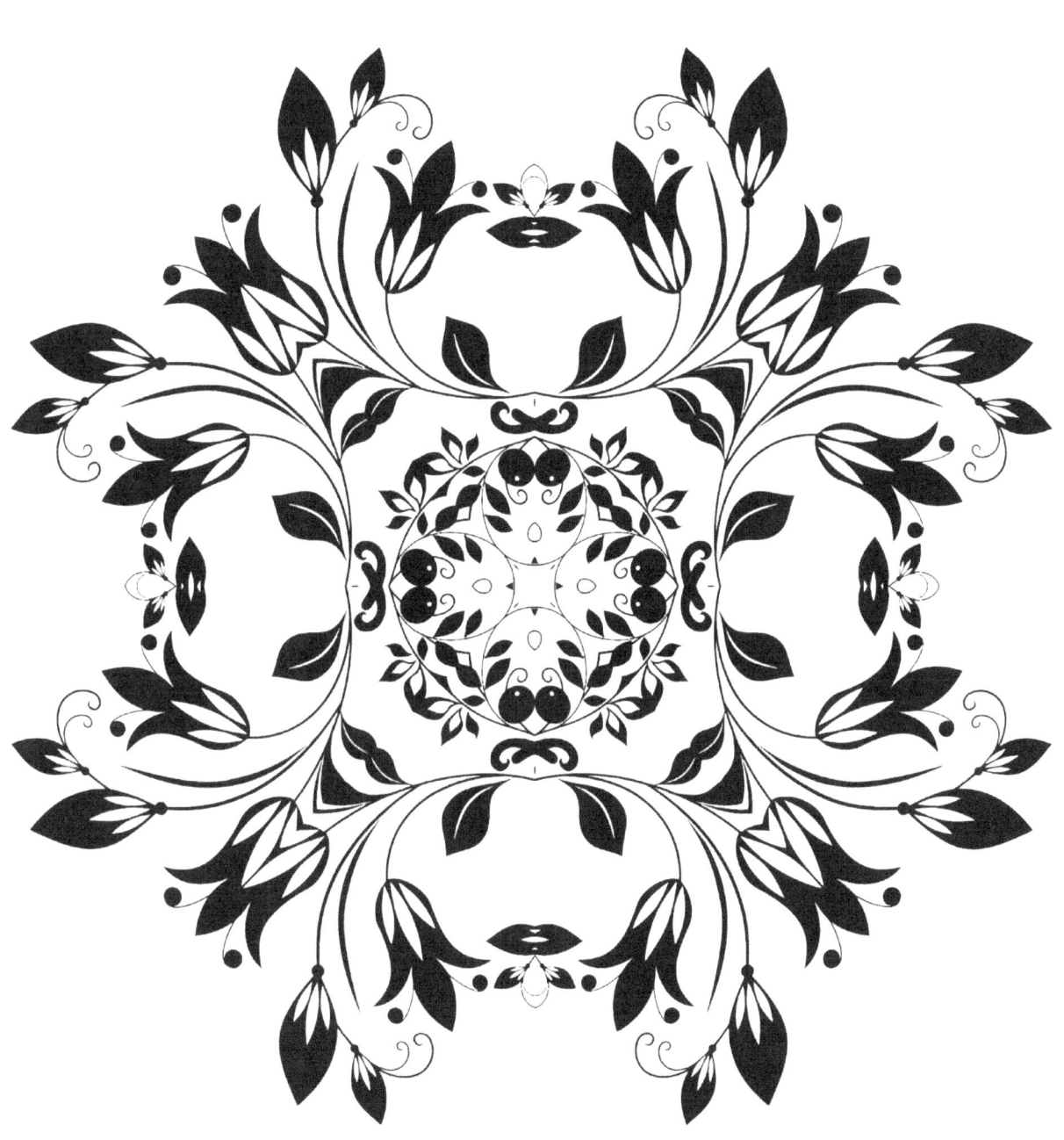

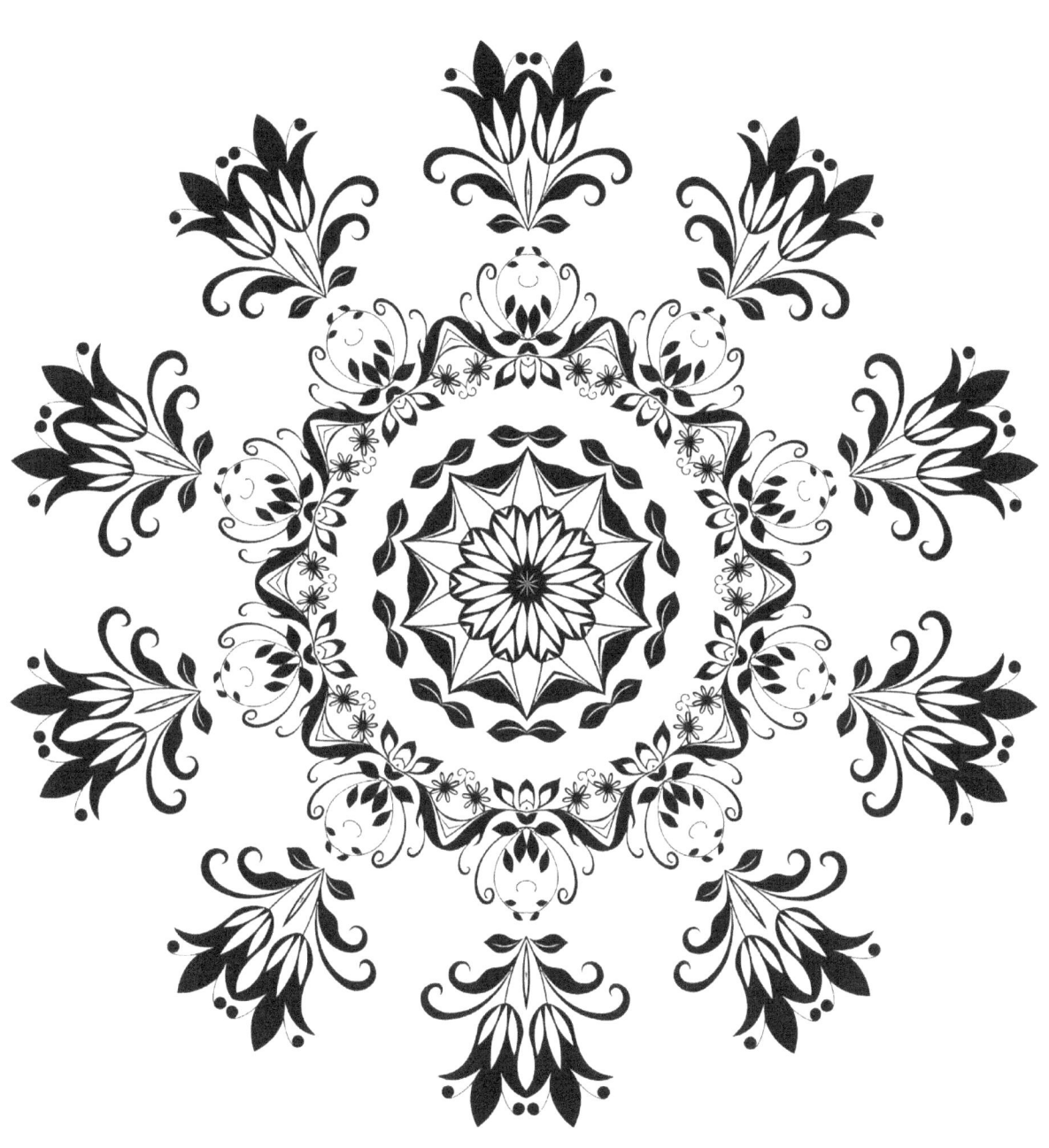

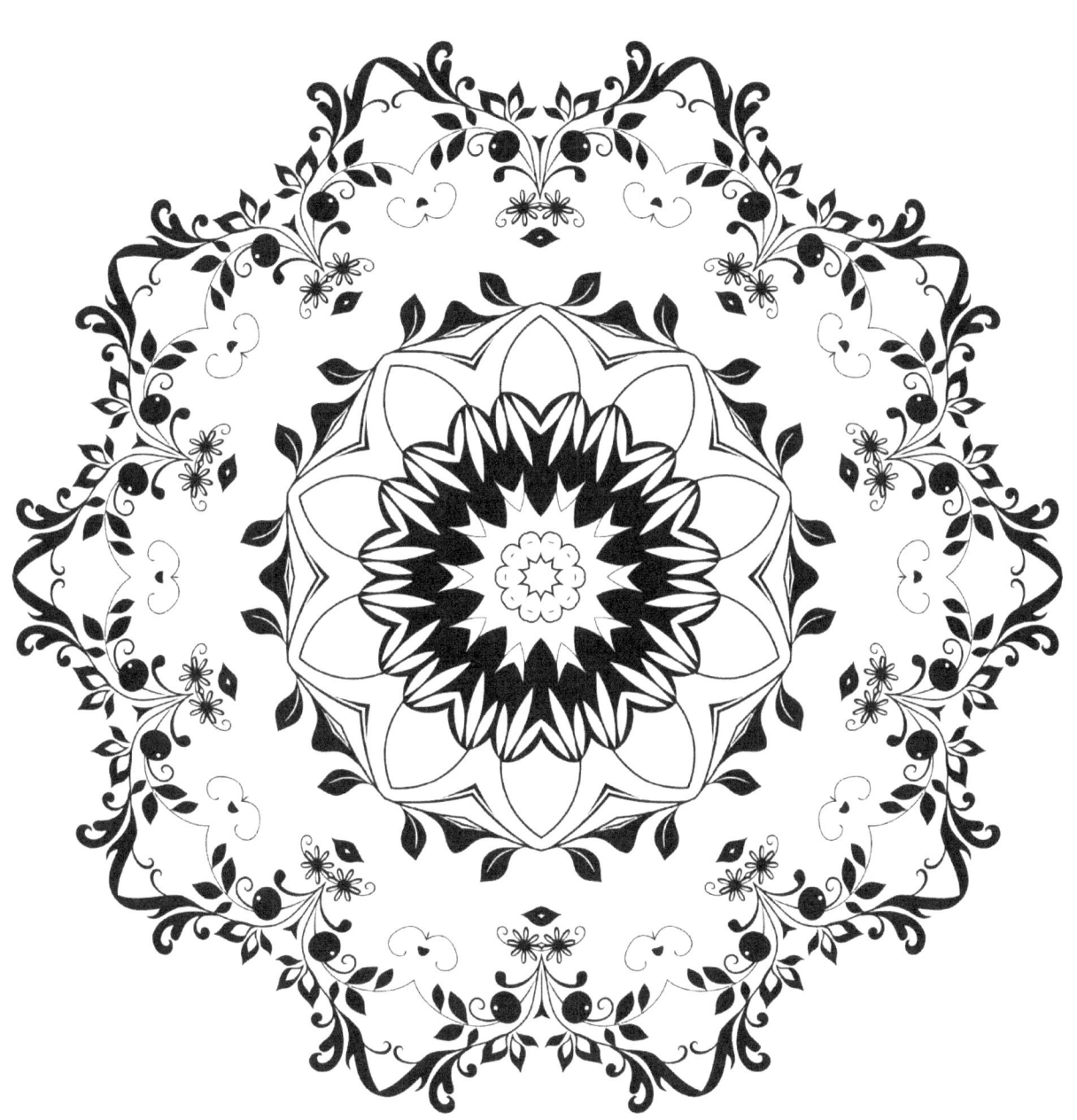

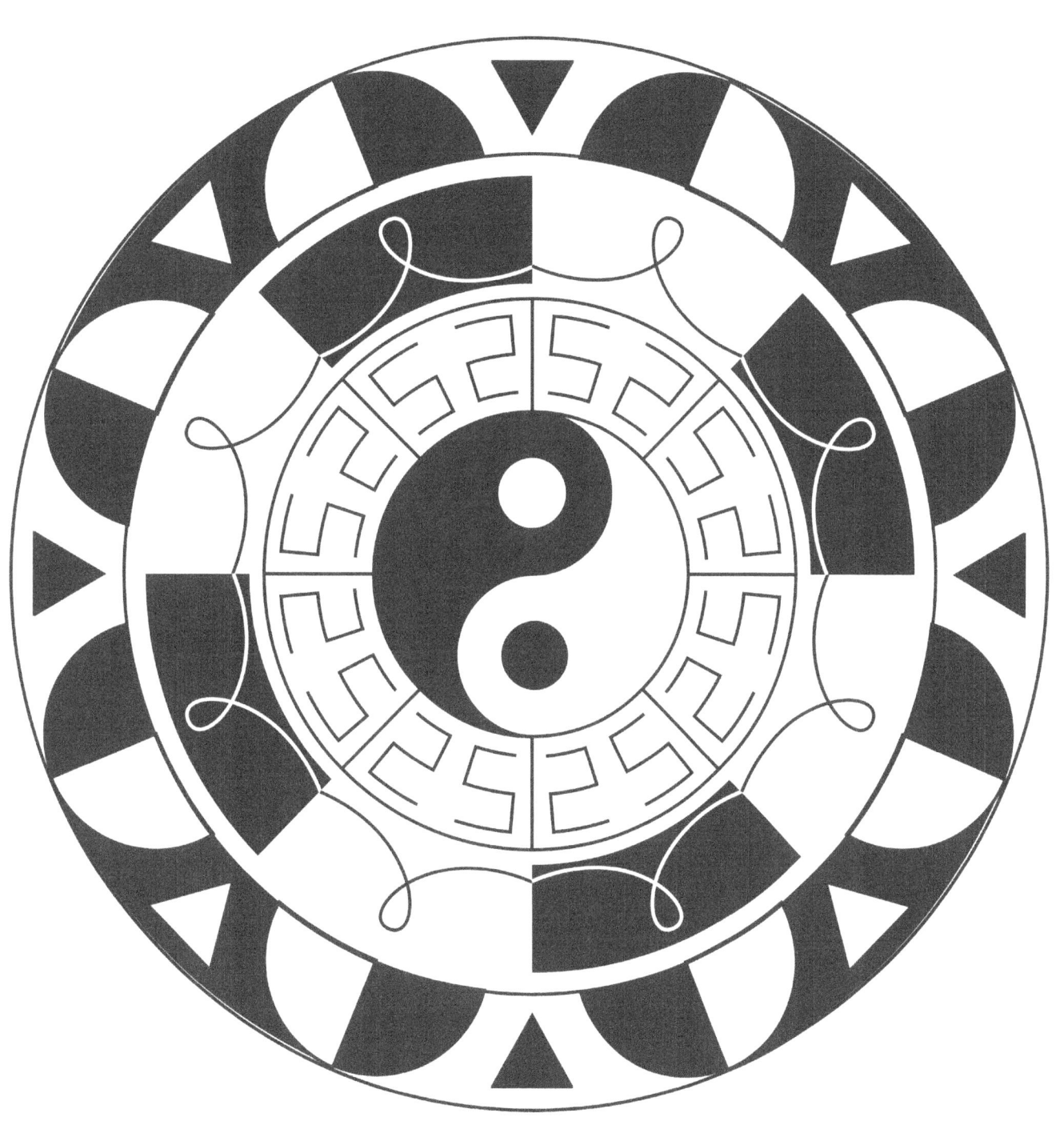

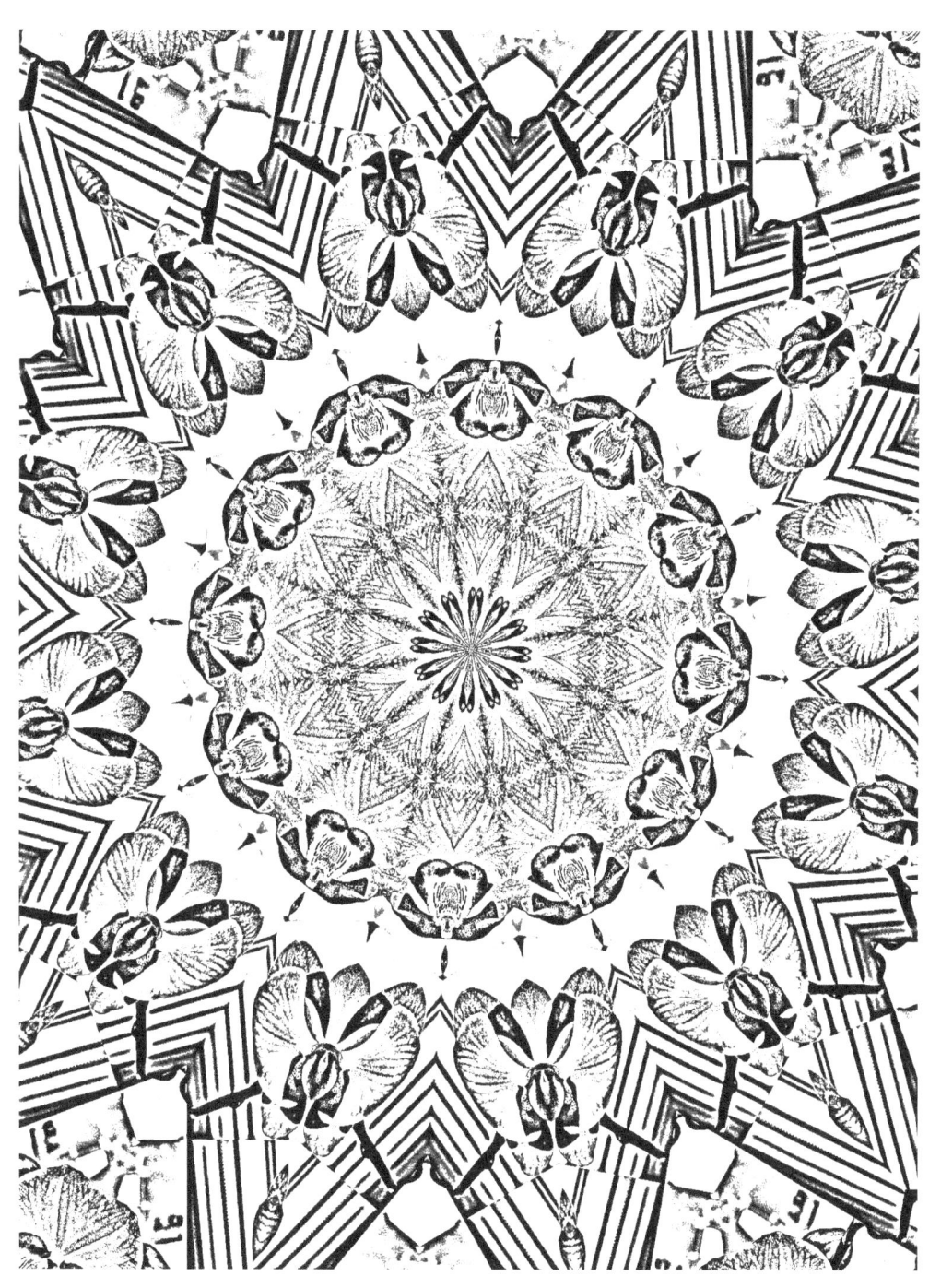

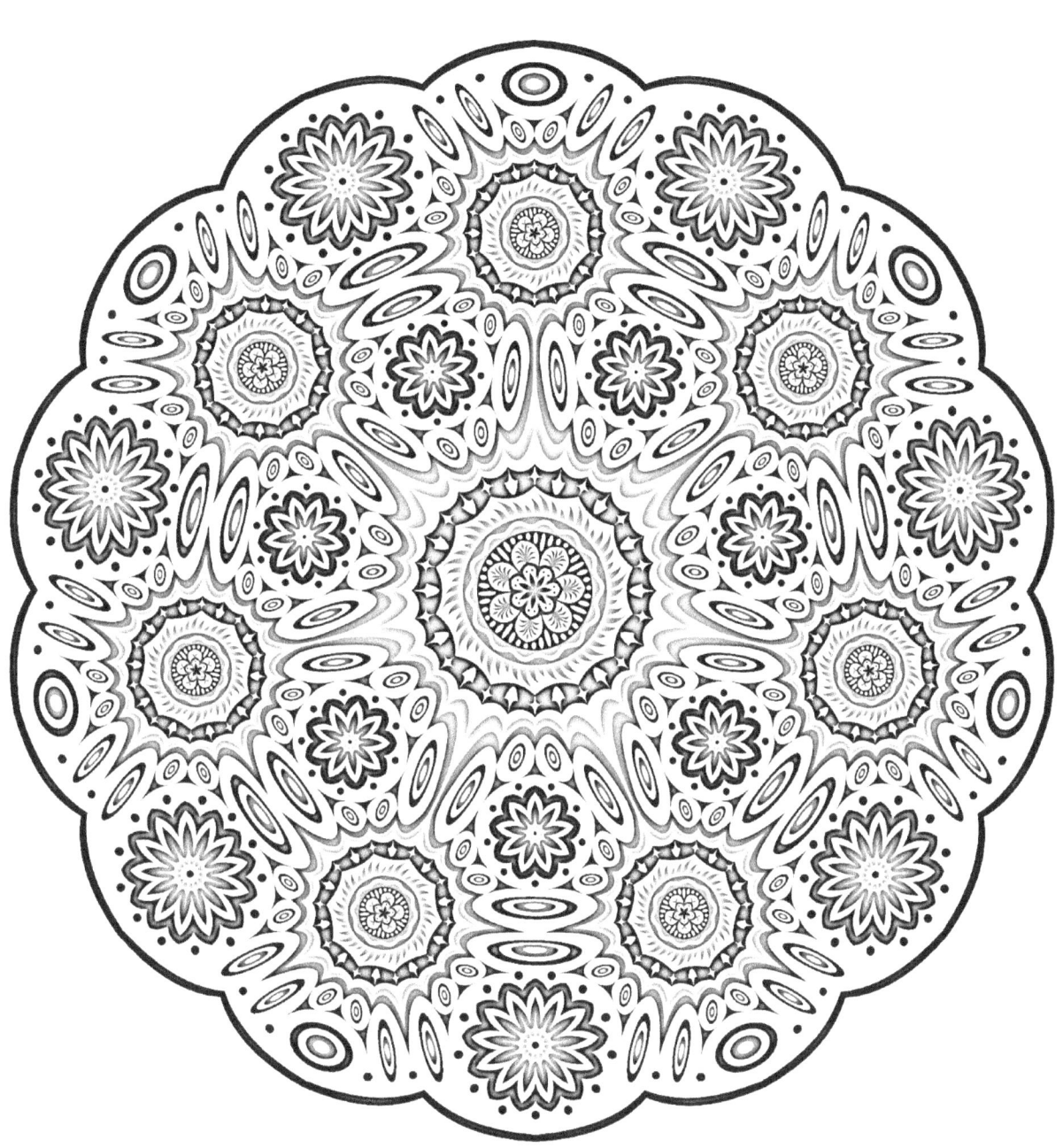

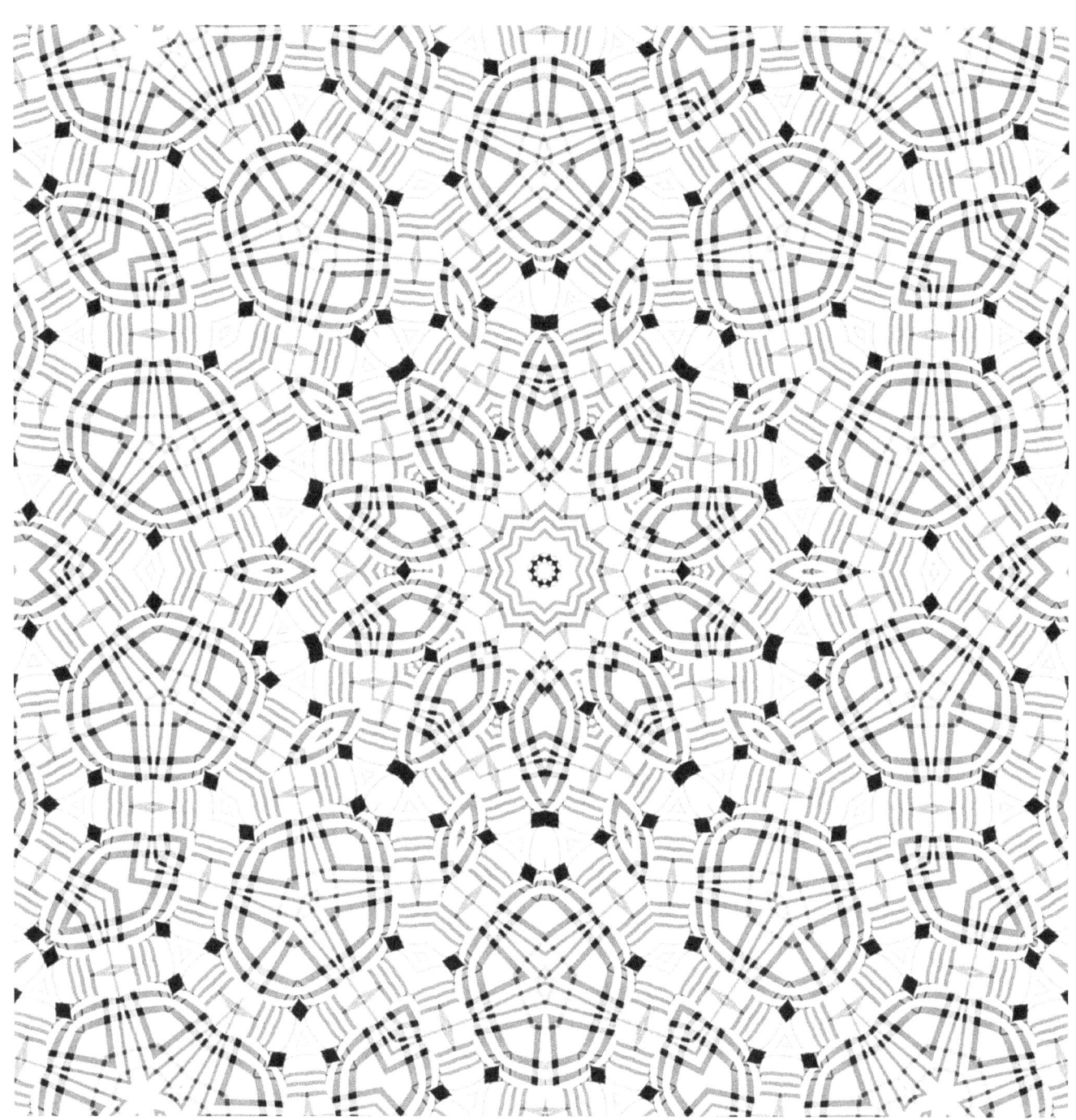

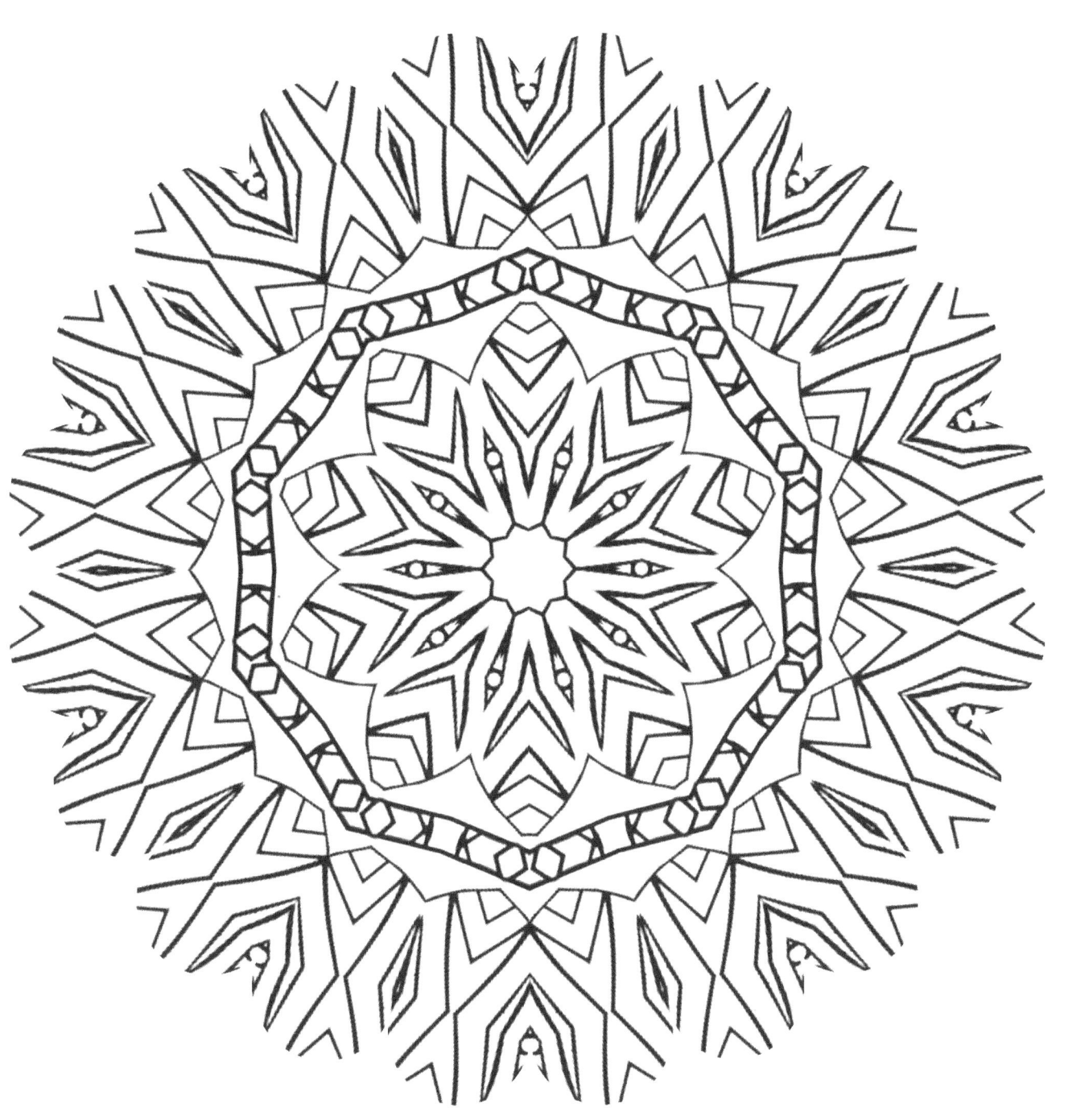

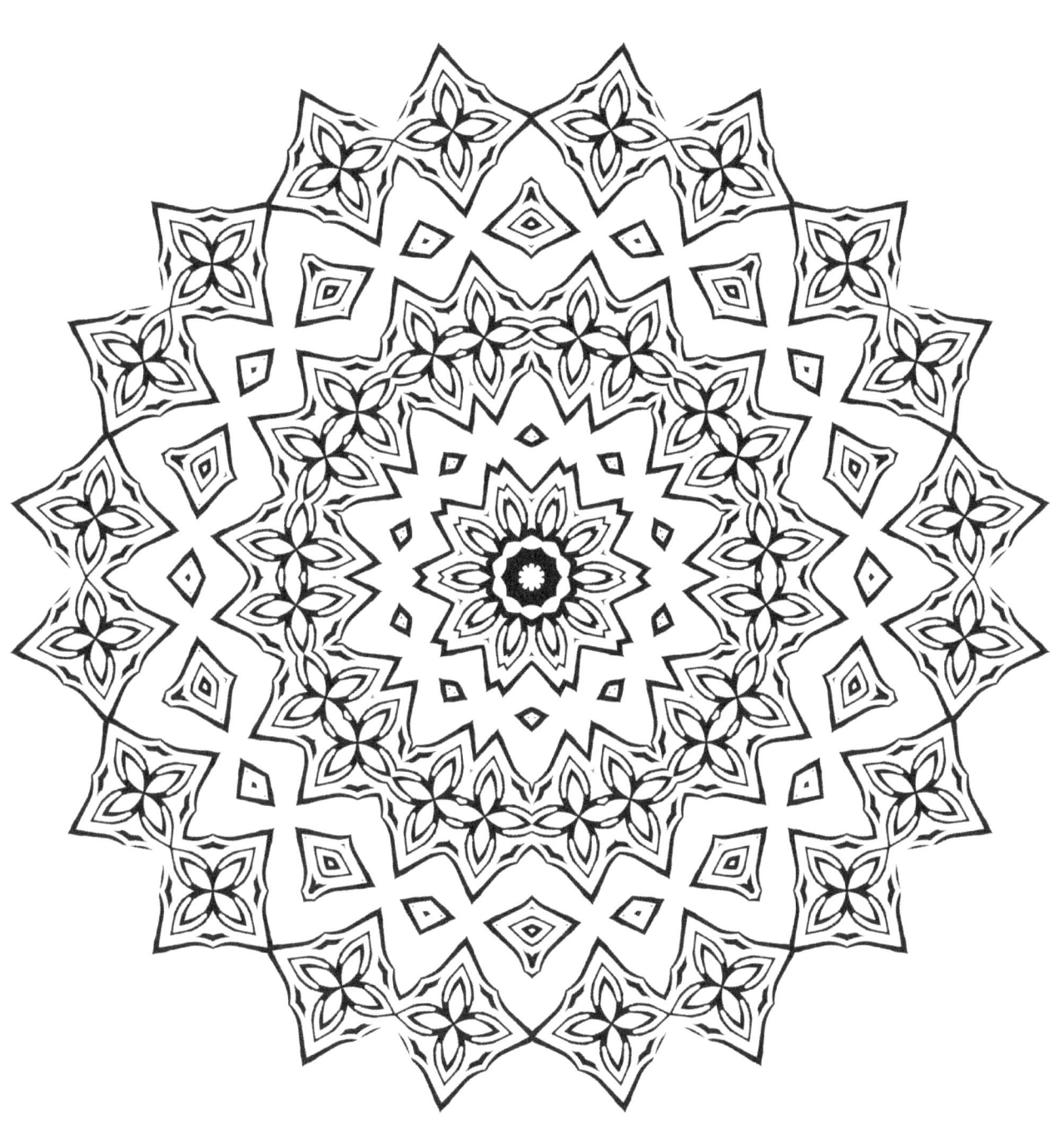

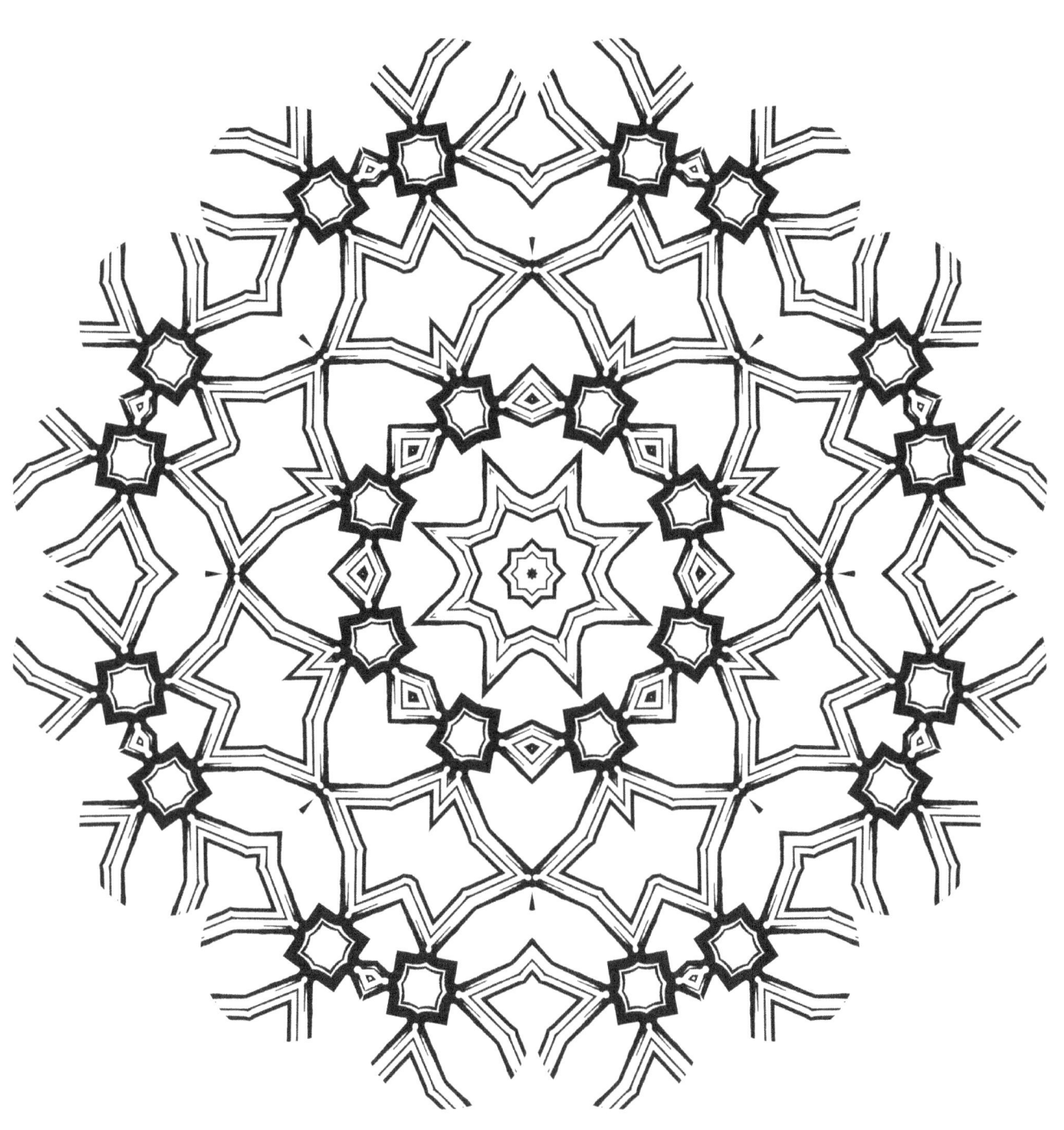

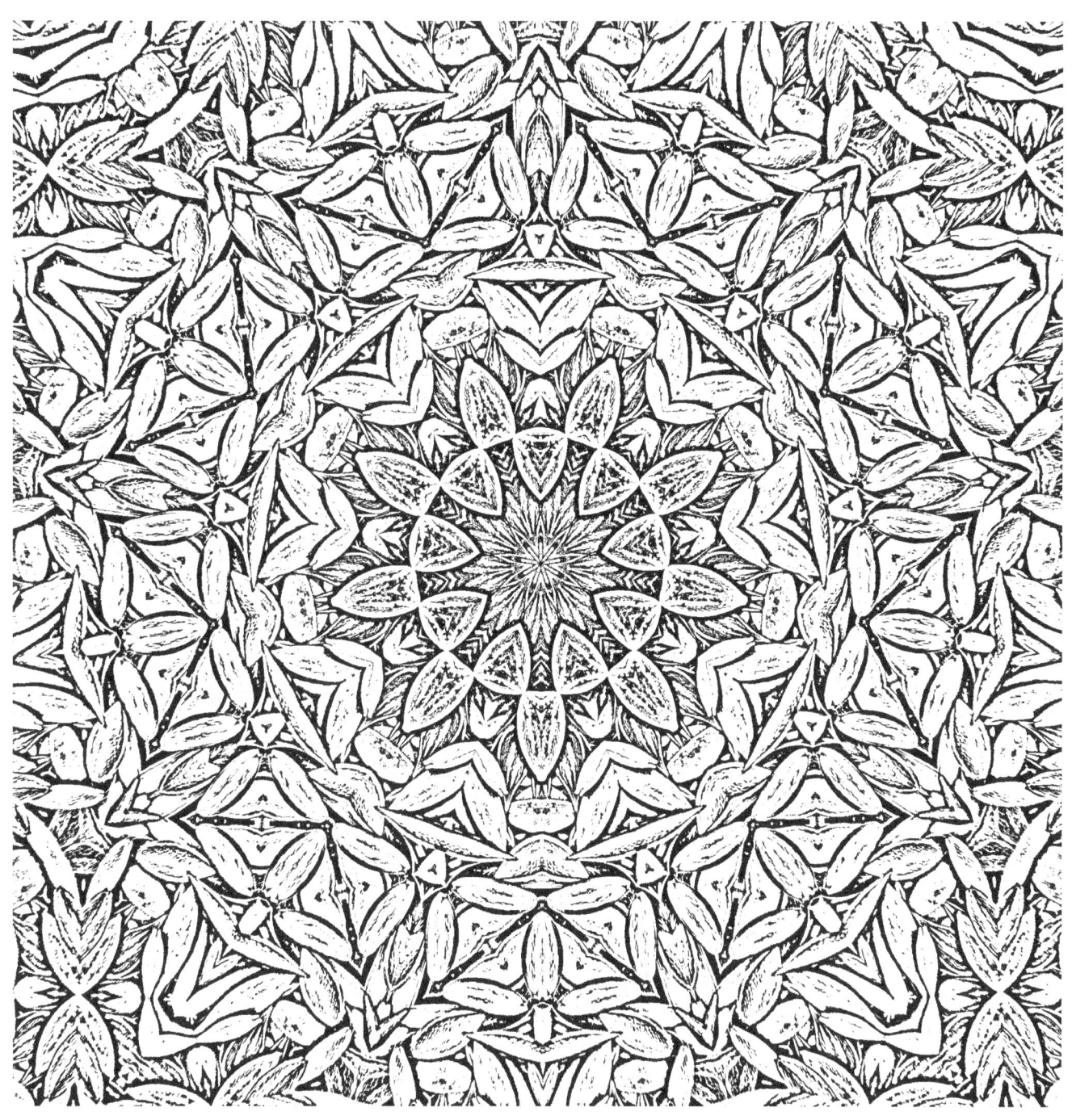

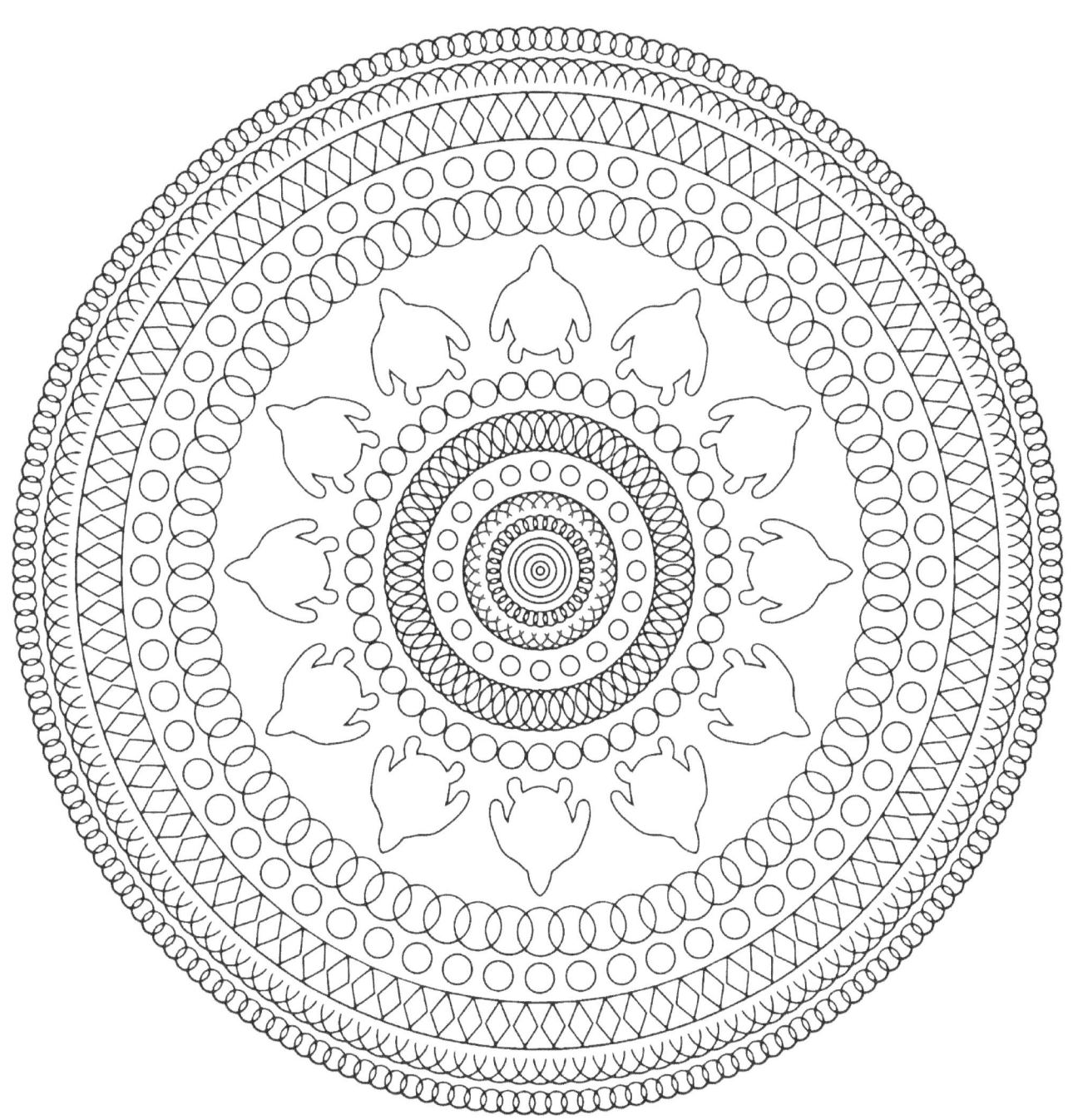

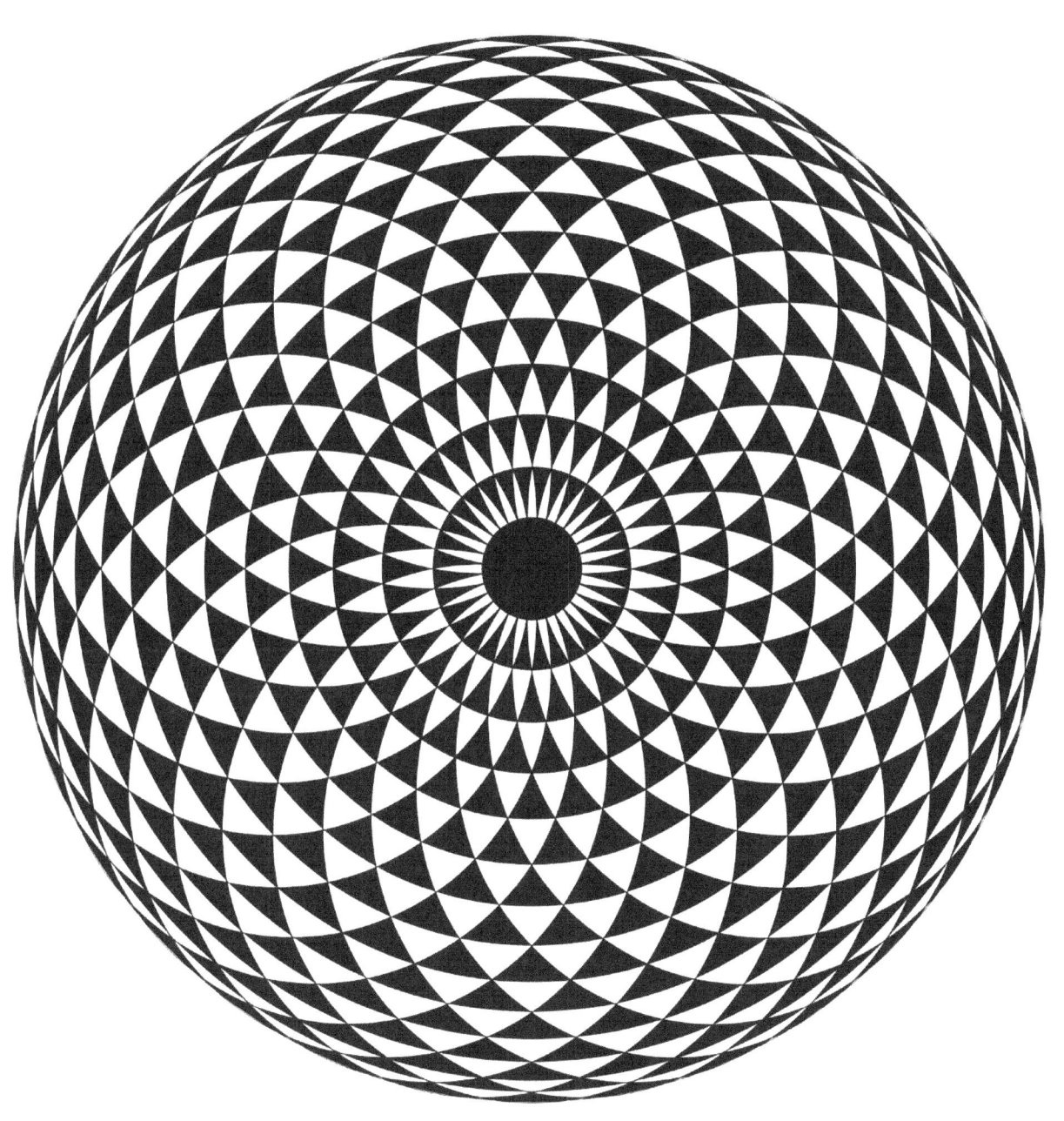

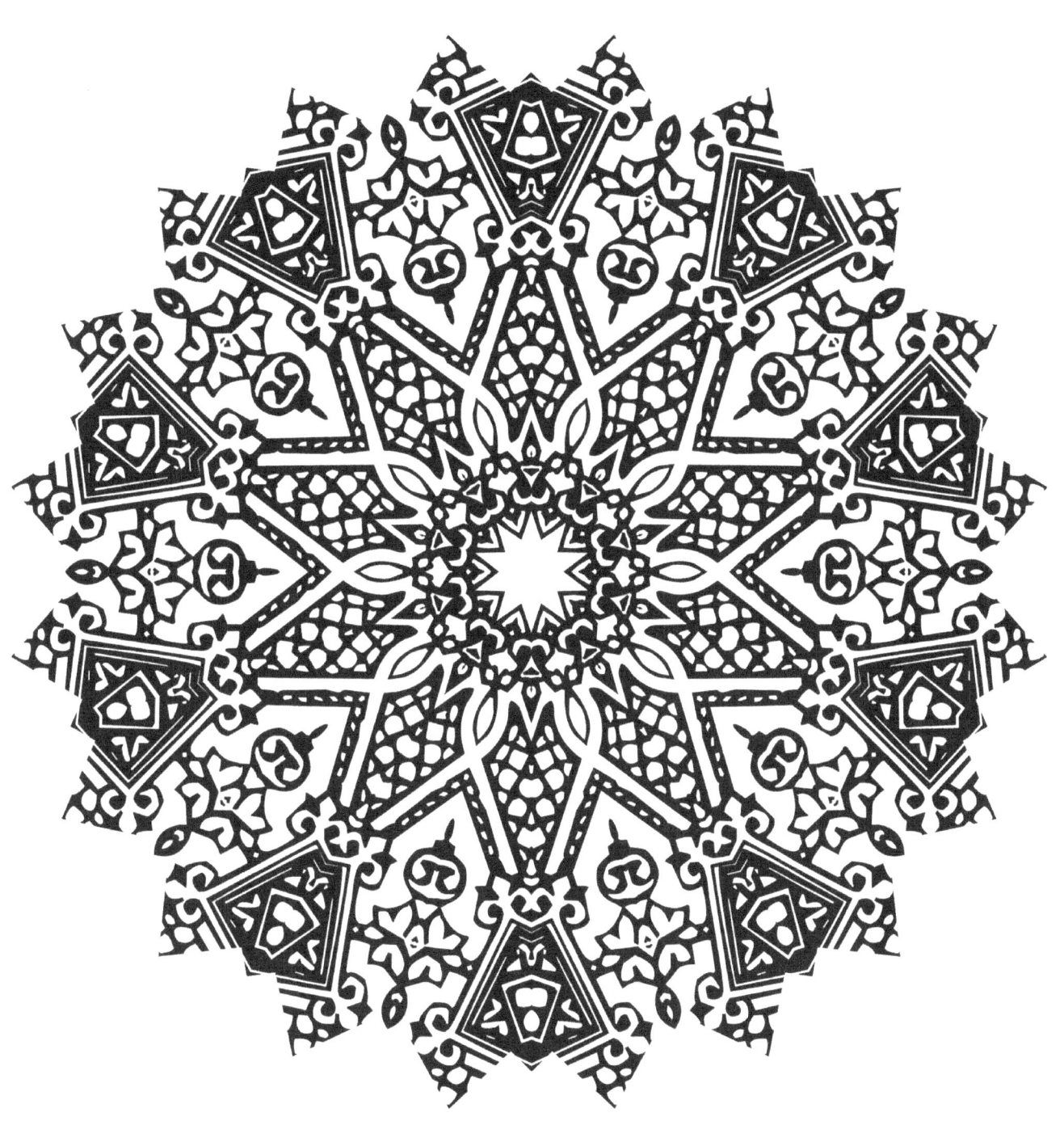

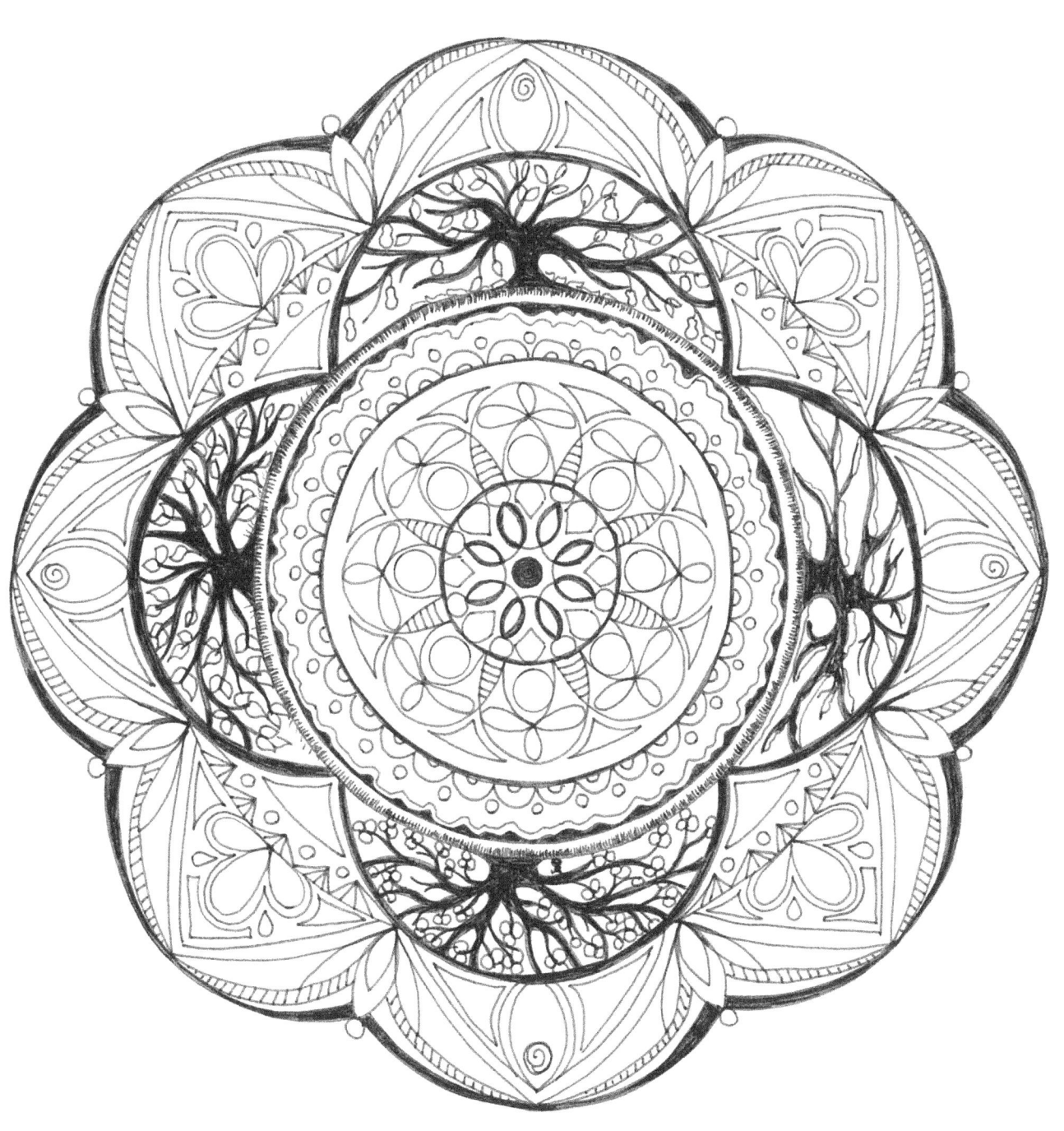

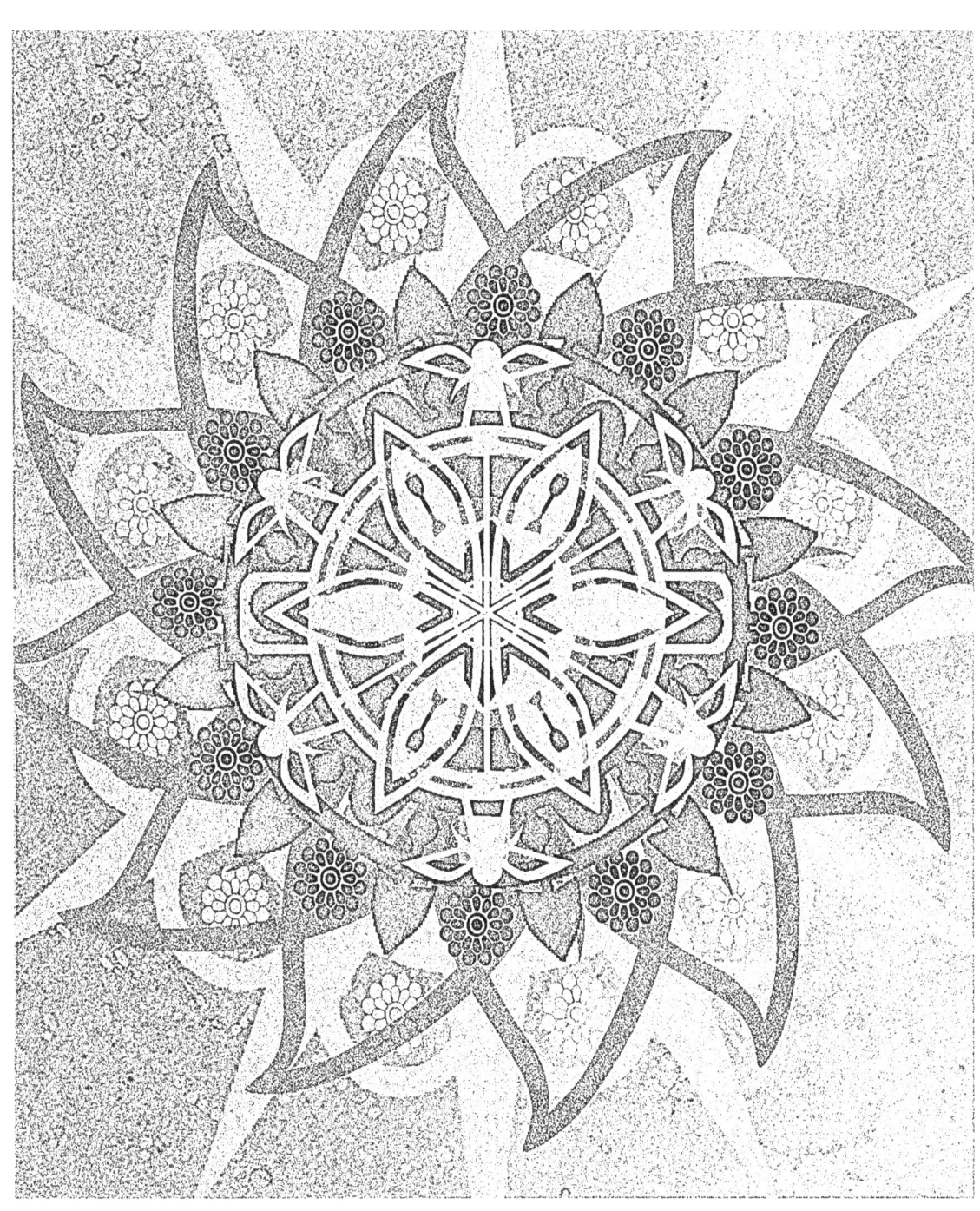

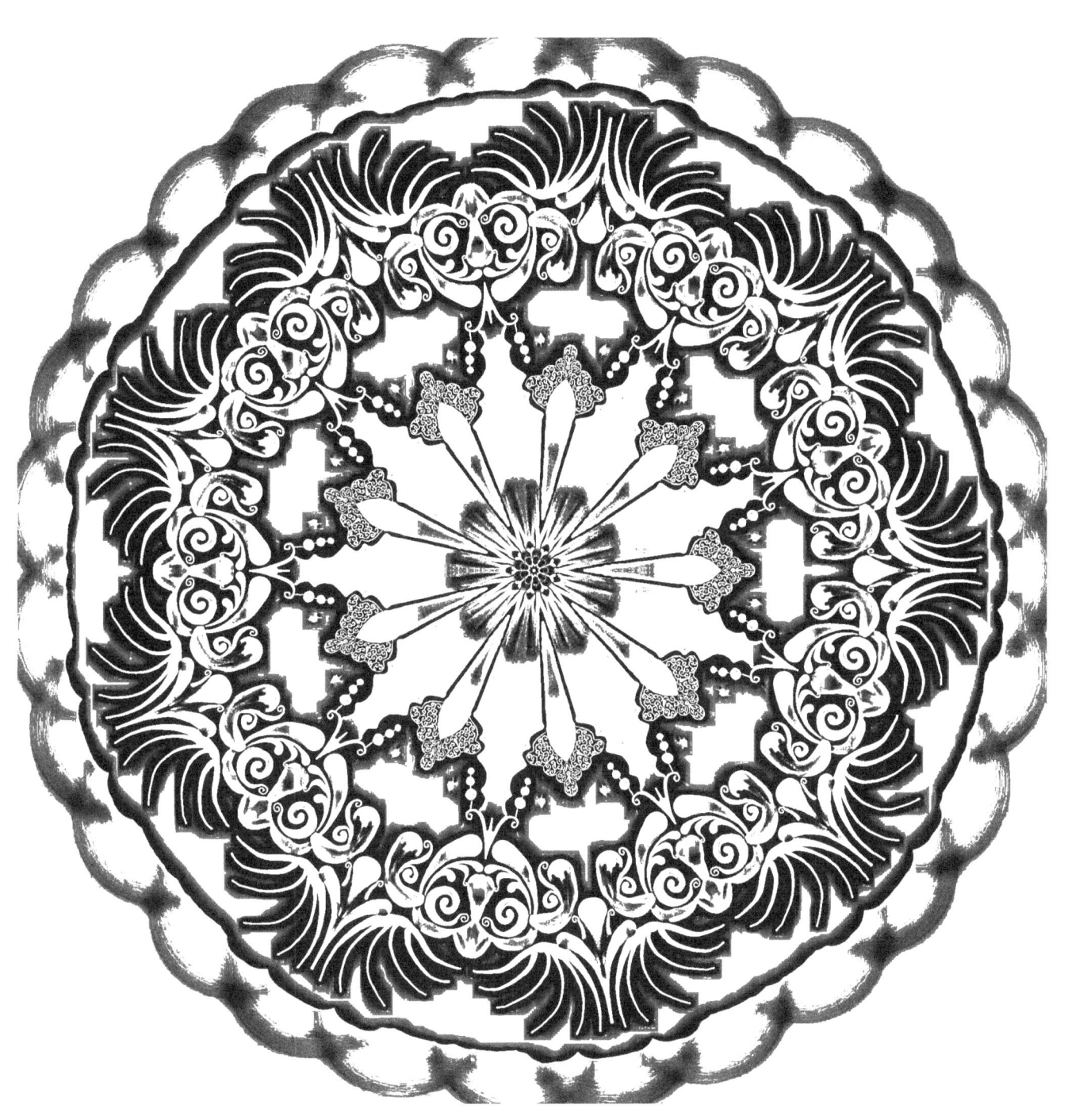

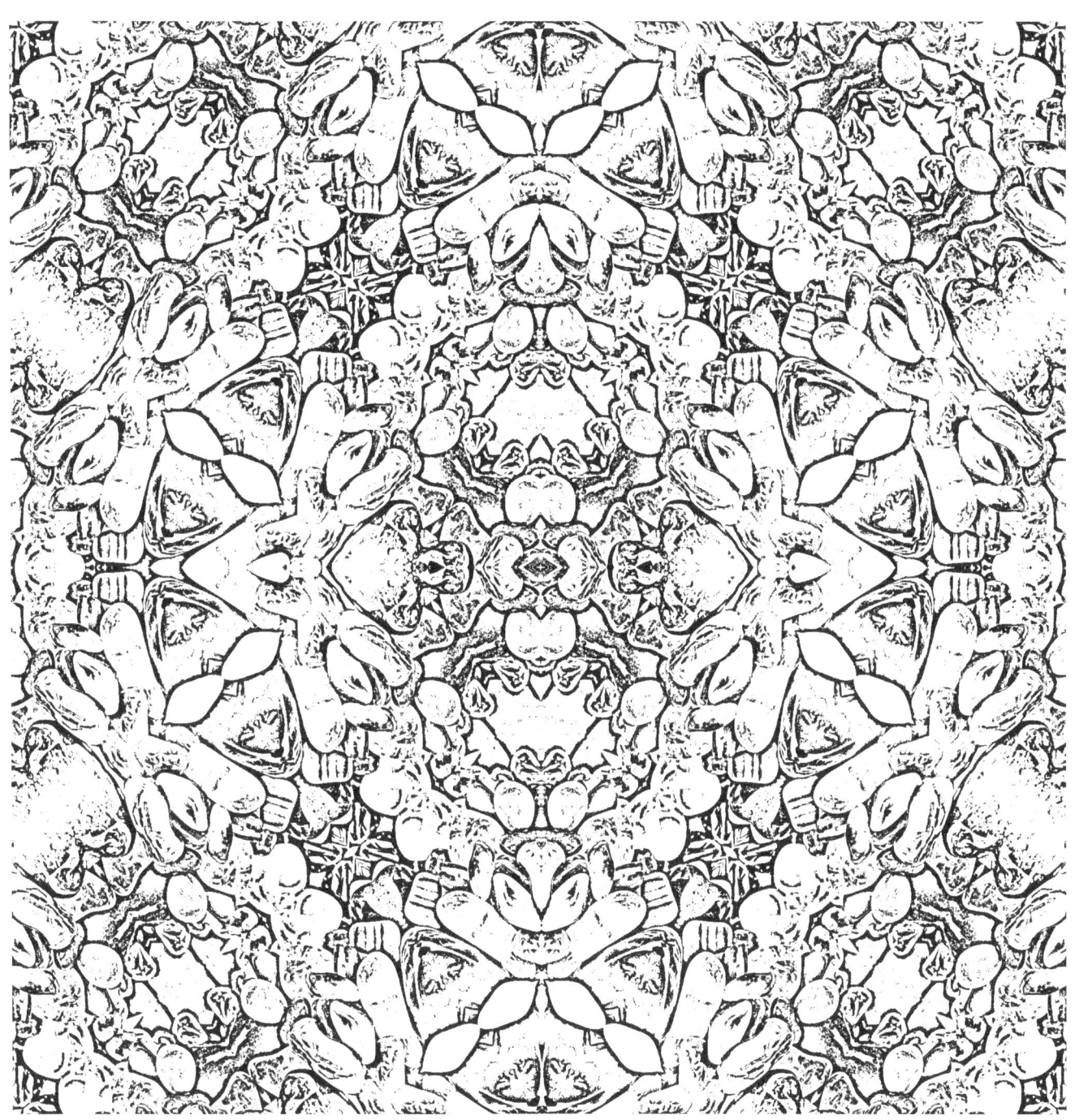

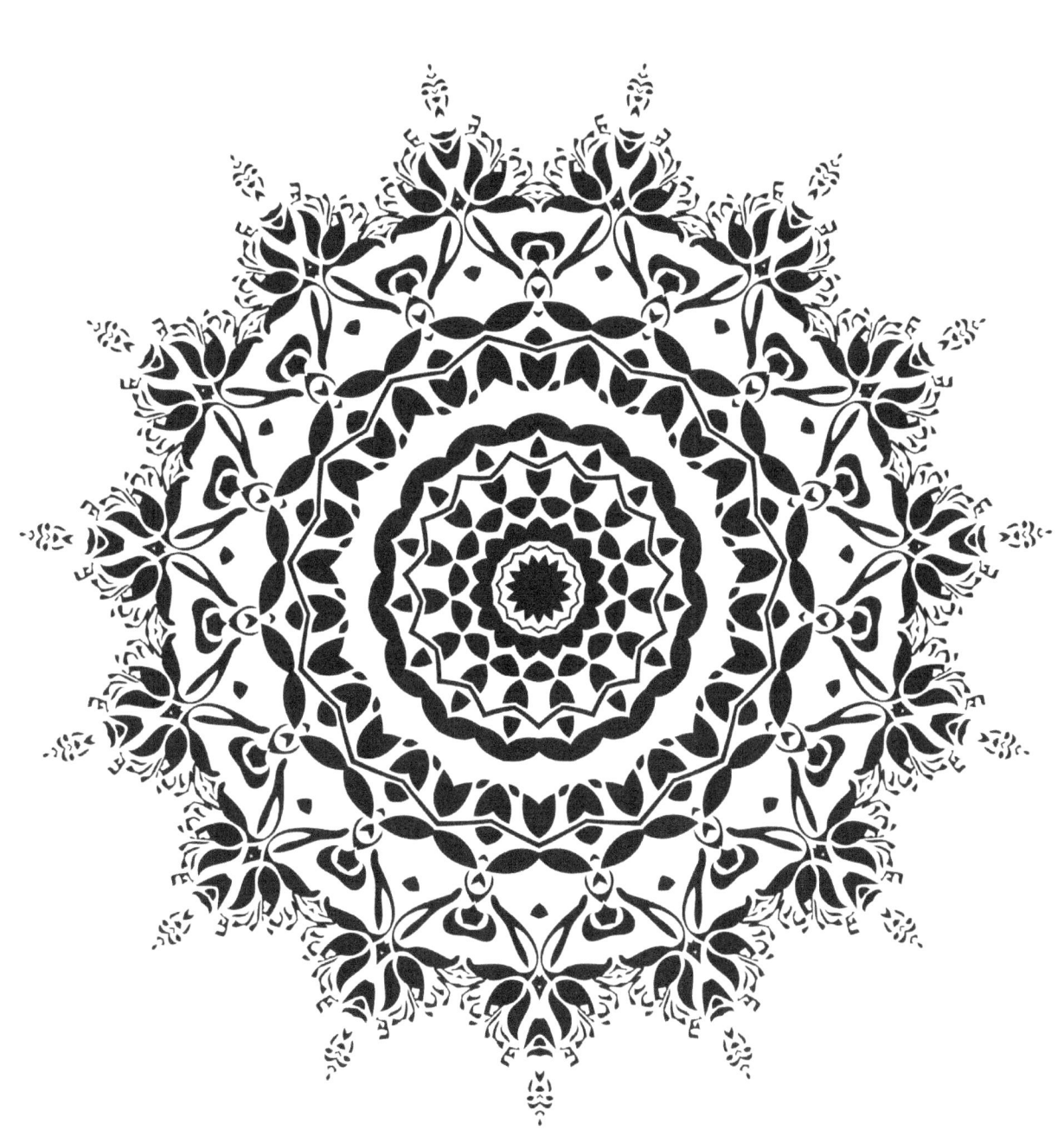

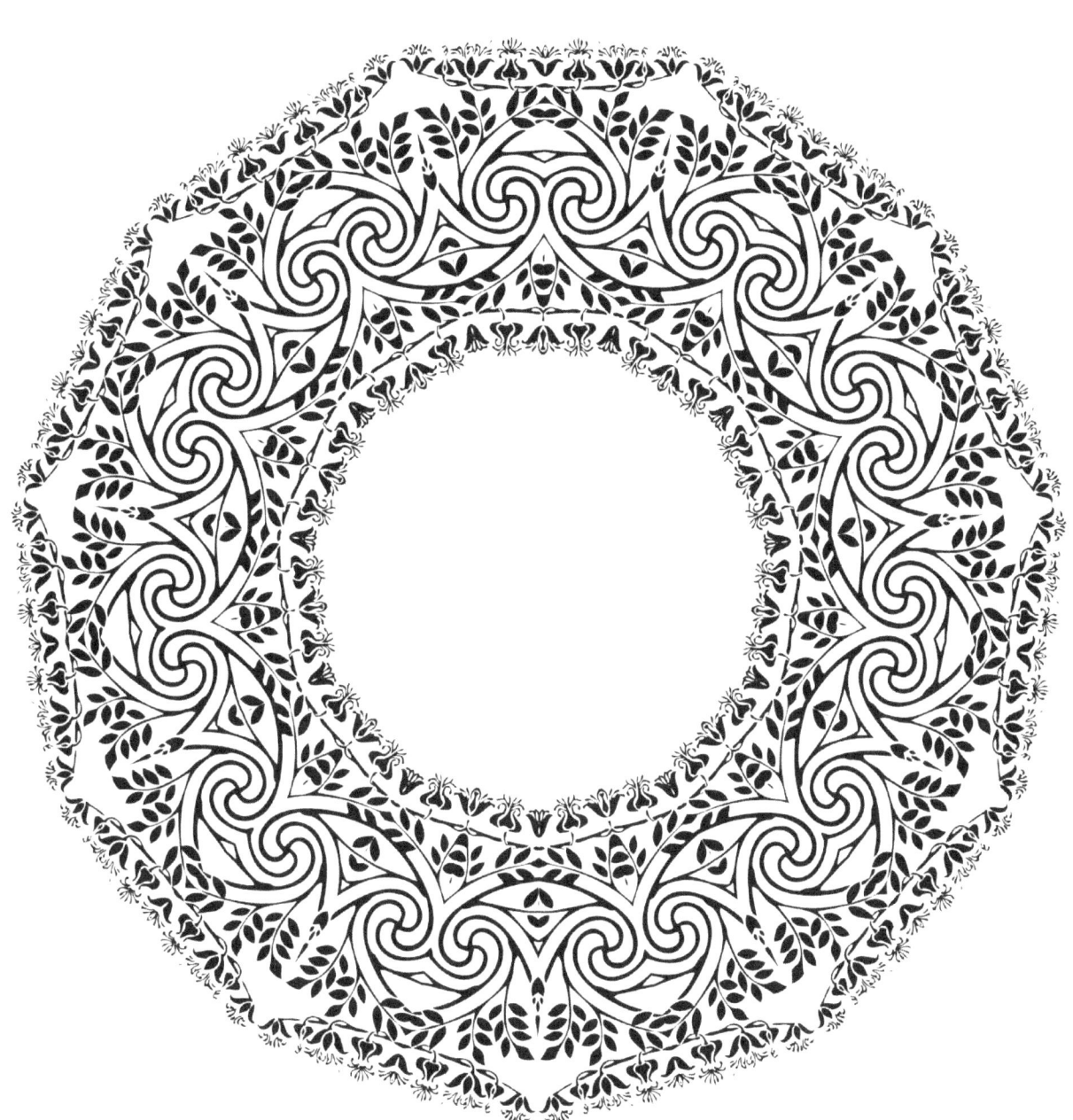

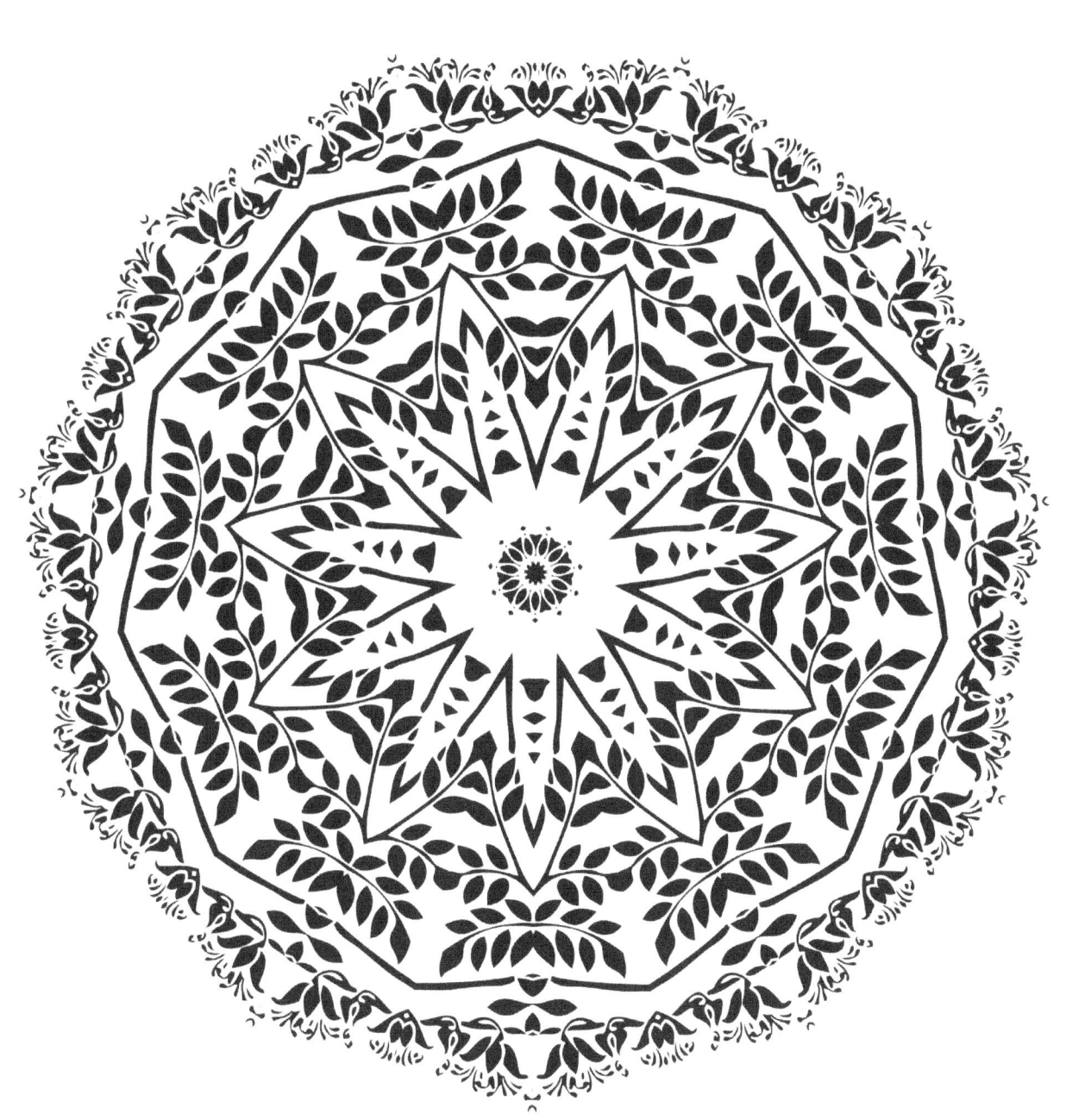

"If you enjoyed this book, don't forget to leave a review on Amazon! This way others can enjoy this book too!
I'm just a home based author with NO "big marketing company" behind me, so I highly appreciate your reviews, and it only takes a minute to do.

To submit a review:
1. Just go to Amazon and under the BOOKS category, search this book's title *"Bring Me To Life Coloring Book: Mandala"* to get to the product detail page for this book on Amazon.
2. Click **Write a customer review** in the Customer Reviews section.
3. Click **Submit**.

Thank you in advance for submitting!"

www.ingramcontent.com/pod-product-compliance
Lightning Source LLC
Chambersburg PA
CBHW080724190526
45169CB00006B/2511